# Girls' Life

# ULTIMATE
# Guide to Surviving
# Middle School

From the creators of
*Girls' Life magazine*
Edited by Lauren Brown

Scholastic Inc.
New York   Toronto   London   Auckland   Sydney
Mexico City   New Delhi   Hong Kong

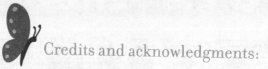 

## Credits and acknowledgments:

Here's to Karen Bokram and her amazing team of *Girls' Life* writers and editors for their contributions to this book including Katie Abbondanza, Amanda Forr, Kristen Kemp, Jiae Kim, Patricia McNamara, Lisa Mulcahy, Laura Sandler, and Michelle Silver.

ISBN 978-0-545-20235-0

Copyright © 2010 by Girls' Life

Published by Scholastic Inc.
SCHOLASTIC and associated logos are trademarks and/or registered trademarks of Scholastic Inc.

12 11 10 9 8 7 6 5 4 3 2 1                    10 11 12 13 14 15/0

illustrated by Bill Thomas and Dynamo Limited
Designed by Two Red Shoes Design                    40
Printed in the U.S.A.
First printing, April 2010

# CONTENTS

# Introduction

**Welcome** to middle school! For lots of girls, this means a new building, new teachers, new activities, and even making some new friends. It's totally normal to be thinking of middle school as **an amazing adventure** . . . and one of the scariest things that's ever happened to you. (Yeah, both at the same time.)

**But the reality is,** you're so not alone in this. Your *bestie* is thinking the exact same thoughts. So is the most popular girl in school. And the smartest kid in your grade. Literally, every single person you went to class with last year is worried, and excited and completely freaked out about starting middle school this year. Who knew you all had so much in common?

Middle school is going to toss a few challenges your way, that's for sure. But trust us when we tell you it's nothing you can't handle—we promise! And lucky for you, **GL has your back.** We know what's stressin' you out most—**homework overload, scary teachers, mean girls, fitting in** . . . oh, and did we mention boys? This book has all the tips and tricks you need to make your middle school years your best yet. **You're gonna be great, girl!** (And you might want to think about passing this book on to your BFF when you're through. Seriously, she's as nervous as you are!)

Here at *GL*, we always have just **one person** in mind when we create each one of these books: you. And, like any good friend, we're always open to suggestions. We asked over 1,000 *GL* girls what you most wanted to see in this book. And, girls, did you have answers . . .

"How to not get lost in a huge school. And how to keep your grade school friends close. And how to get organized!"—*Emily J., Colorado*

"Give us tips to boost our confidence!" *Georgia W., Indiana*

"How do I get good grades and still have a social life? How do I balance it all?"—*Hilary K., Florida*

That's why we've gathered the **best advice** on everything from cliques to classes and put it into these pages. While we can't promise you exactly what the next two or three years will bring (New friends? New crush? The lead in the play?) there is **ONE** thing we can guarantee—things are going to change in your world.

I remember lying in bed the night before *middle school,* kind of excited but also thinking; "Nothing will ever be the same again." Sure, most of my best friends were going to my school. I knew some of the older kids. Heck, I even knew a couple teachers. **But,** somehow, I also knew things would be different. Classes would be harder, my friends would make other new friends (and I would, too), and we'd all suddenly be pulled in a **million new directions**. It's easy to stress out thinking about all that. But here's the thing: You only get one shot at this school year. And, as hard as it is to imagine, *someday* you won't be in school. We at *GL* want you to be able to look back and think about all the great things that happened because you took chances and rolled with the changes.

# The Big Switch

**S**ummer sped by in a snap (sigh . . .) and all of a sudden it's time to gear up for the first day of middle school. No doubt you're stressed. Maybe you're worried you'll forget your locker combo. Or that you'll get lost in the halls. Or maybe you're just sweatin' about what to wear on that first day. But guess what? It would be weirder if you *weren't* nervous once August rolls around.

But we've got some great news for ya: *Middle school* is so much cooler than elementary. Not only will you have way more options for fun (like dances, sports, and all of the extracurrics you want!), but you'll also have tons of variety in your day.

No longer will you be confined to one classroom for eight hours—now you'll be shifting gears every forty-five minutes or so as you switch from science to Spanish and everything in between. Okay, so you may not have recess anymore, but you'll still be able to kick it with your friends at lunch. Freaking out because all of your friends have completely clashing schedules? *Don't worry,* you'll have plenty of chances to chat up new pals in middle school (while squeezing your usual crew in before and after school and between classes, of course). Feeling better yet? Good!

7

# "YOUR BIGGEST MIDDLE SCHOOL PROBS SOLVED!"

## WHAT IF I GET LOST, AND I'M LATE FOR CLASS?

**Okay,** so yeah, your new middle school is going to seem huge at first. Take a deep breath and remember that learning your way around a new school takes practice. After just a few weeks, you'll be able to get from class to class blindfolded if you had to.

But if you don't want to look like a lost puppy on the *first day,* then make it your business to get your mom or dad to take you over to the school in advance. **Many schools** open about a week before classes start, so grab your schedule and visit your school one afternoon. Stop by the front office, and ask for a map. *Walk to each* class in the order of your schedule. And coordinate with your **friends** to see who is in your classes so you can meet and hit the hallways together. And if you do get lost? Just ask a teacher or staff member for directions.

### I WAS COOL AT MY OLD SCHOOL. WHAT IF I'M NOT AT MY NEW SCHOOL? You may

**feel** you don't fit in for a few days, but that makes you one of the *new girls*—not a loser. Rather than focusing on your popularity quotient, concentrate on finding friends that you like and who genuinely like you back. What can be cooler than that?

### WHO SHOULD I SIT WITH ON THE BUS? If rowdy kids

**are** aiming paper footballs at your head in the back of the bus, sit up front. *Take a seat next* to that girl from your math class who seems nice or that kid who was next to you in kindergarten. If you don't recognize anyone those first few days, just find an empty spot and introduce yourself. You'll know everyone soon enough! And here's an insider tip: If you sit in the back, you may take a harder bounce when the driver hits a bump in the road.

### I'M GOING TO MISS MY OLD SCHOOL, TEACHERS, FRIENDS, CLASSES, EVERYTHING! Yes you will. Visit your old school and

friends while you're adjusting to the new faces. And try to keep things in perspective—eventually, you'll look back on middle school, thinking how much you miss it.

# WHAT IF A BIGGER KID TRIES TO START A FIGHT WITH ME?

**We know** it's scary going to school with kids who are bigger. But chances of this actually happening out of the blue are not very likely. The smartest thing to do in this sitch is talk to a teacher.

# WHAT IF SOMEONE OFFERS ME A CIGARETTE OR DRUGS?

**Don't panic,** don't lecture, and don't feel pressured. Simply say, "No, thanks," smile, and be on your merry way. We'll have a lot more on standing up to peer pressure in Chapter 6.

# WHAT IF I WALK INTO THE WRONG CLASSROOM AND MAKE A FOOL OF MYSELF?

**You can go** for laughs and say, "So this is what this room looks like!" Or, you can spin around and exit the room. Simple.

## I DON'T WANT TO BE IN A "BABY GRADE" AGAIN. HOW CAN I HANG WITH OLDER KIDS?

**Get a good** sense of who's in your grade, and try making friends with them first. Instead of seeing it as a "baby grade," think of it as a *chance to interact with kids* who are in the same place as you, experiencing all the new things middle school has to offer. See, you already have something in common!

## SHOULD I BUY OR PACK A LUNCH?

**If you want** to eat healthy (or just can't stand the idea of cardboard pizza or mystery meat for lunch), pack yourself *a nutritious lunch*. If you plan on buying lunch at school, make sure you've got your funds together and in your book bag so you don't forget in the morning.

## WHAT SHOULD I DO IF OLDER KIDS TELL ME OBVIOUS LIES, LIKE, "DID YOU KNOW THERE'S A POOL ON THE FIFTH FLOOR?"

**Shoot them back a line** that says you're nobody's fool. Try, "Yeah, I went for a swim last week. It was great," or, "Isn't it right next to the sauna?" *Then smile and move on.* A word of advice: Do NOT buy an elevator pass!

# 4 No-fail ways to remember your locker combination!

☀ Buy your lock a week before school, and keep it by your bed. Practice it over and over for five minutes every morning and night.

☀ Write your combo down fifteen times, twice a day for a week!

☀ Make up a rhyme. Say your combo is 42-6-33: "My favorite number is 42/My 6-year-old sister plays peek-a-boo/I have 33 cows that go moo-moo-moo." Hokey, but it works!

☀ If all else fails, write it in permanent marker inside your backpack.

# ✿ GETTING PREPPED

Of course, there's a lot more to middle school than interacting with upperclassmen and navigating your way through the hallways. You're probably also concerned with a ton of other stuff, like how you look, your grades, and how you're going to stay organized when you're just so busy.

## A COUPLE OF WEEKS BEFORE THE FIRST DAY

✳ *Get supplies.* Most of you get lists that let you know what supplies you'll be needing for the school year (book bag, notebooks, pens/pencils, paper, binder, folders, etc.), so take that along when you go school shopping and check off each item as you get it.

**TIP:** Other things you might want to get that just might save the day: Tide to Go stick (for those unfortunate lunch mishaps), compact tampons (to stick in your purse for emergencies), and a mirror for your locker or purse (no more salad-stuck-in-teeth embarrassing moments here).

✳ **Get at least one amazing addition for your closet.** Everyone needs *new stuff* to start off the year. Grab your mom, sister, BFF, or any other fashionista you can find and go shopping for some fab clothes you feel super-confident in. Nothing attracts attention like that glow of inner self-confidence!

**TIP:** If you can't afford to shell out money for new stuff, raid a friend's closet. We've seen our clothes a million times so they seem boring to us. Borrow an outfit to spice up your wardrobe!

✳ **Get great skin.**
If you don't already have a good skin care routine, get one. Nothing is worse than waking up on the first day of school with a huge zit on your face.

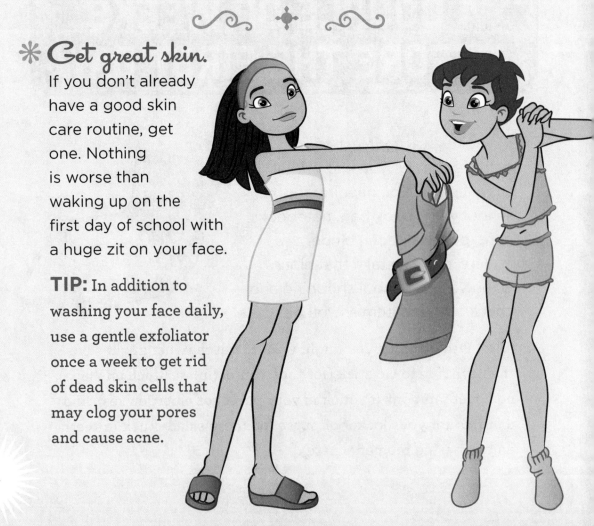

**TIP:** In addition to washing your face daily, use a gentle exfoliator once a week to get rid of dead skin cells that may clog your pores and cause acne.

# NIGHT BEFORE THE FIRST DAY

✳ **Practice a new hairstyle and/or makeup routine.** Once you have the perfect outfit and amazing skin, you'll need to figure out what to do with your hair and makeup. To keep morning *stress at a minimum* on your first day, plan out what you're going to do a few days before the big day and practice it.

**TIP:** Time how long it takes to do the whole routine so you know when to get up in the morning.

✳ **Get your books together.** Gather your binder or notebooks for your classes, and get your book bag ready to go in the morning.

**TIP:** Color code! Use your red folder and notebook for one class, your blue folder and notebook for another, and so forth. It makes it easy to grab and go. Hey, there isn't that much time between classes!

✳ **Study your schedule.** Especially if you're starting at a new school, you'll want to know where you're going and when so you're not late.

TIP: Like we said before, don't be afraid to ask someone for directions if you're a little lost—or just want to introduce yourself to that cute boy standing next to your locker!

✳ **Lay out your clothes.** Get your new outfit ready so you don't have to *waste time* deciding what to wear in the A.M. If your clothes need to be ironed, do that before you go to bed.

✳ **Set your alarm!** Even if your mom or dad wakes you up in the morning, get used to *setting an alarm* and getting yourself up. Use Mom and Dad as backup.

✳ **Make a checklist.** To make sure you don't forget anything, *compile a list of everything* you'll need in your hands when you walk out the door—book bag (which you should already have filled with the essentials), lunch/lunch money, schedule, etc.

Being prepped doesn't stop once you're supplied, scrubbed, and sporting some cute clothes. To start the year off right, here are some things to think about crossing off your to-do list.

# 5 things NOT to do on your first day of school

☀ DON'T be over the top. Confidence is a definite plus, but be sure not to strut into the first day with too much attitude.

☀ DON'T be someone you're not. Nothing says, "I have no self-esteem," louder than being a copycat or a "yes" girl. Just be you. That's good enough.

☀ DON'T worry about the little slipups. If you find yourself in an embarrassing moment, brush it off. You'll probably be the only one to remember it.

☀ DON'T make any quick decisions about your new school or teachers. You need to get the lay of the land on everything.

☀ DON'T freak out. As you get older, the work is meant to get harder. We're not gonna lie—more is expected of you. You're also going to be in a new setting. Stay calm, and give yourself the chance to adjust. You can do it!

## THE BOTTOM LINE . . .

Your brain may be bogged down with details right now, but as you start up school, remember that, despite the stress, these next few years are actually going to be fun. So make a conscious effort to enjoy every minute of the first day. Get really psyched over which clubs to join. LOL at lunch with your BFF. Stake out a spot in the hallway to check out the boys. Stay in the moment and the first day of school will help you get fired up about the entire school year!

# FIRST WEEK MUST-DOS

## ☆ Reboot Your Routine

Studies show that if you change up the way you do ho-hum tasks, it can actually *re-train your brain* to feel happier. Mixing up your daily routine ups your energy, helps you see new ways to solve probs, and gets you truly diggin' on your day. So . . . if you walk to school, go a **different route** now and then. In the habit of grabbin' a window seat in every classroom? Park yourself front row center— and take notes in purple ink instead of boring blue. Could there be an *easier way to get a new perspective* right from day one?

## ☆ Decide to Do Your Best

Know how there's always one class that makes your eyes glaze—and your grade usually shows it? Vow now not to go on autopilot. Throw yourself into your least-fave class with enthusiasm and find one thing you like about it. Once you've found your hook, stay on track. You might even find yourself *looking forward* to this class.

## ☆ Talk to 5 New Kids

You wouldn't trade your crew for the world—duh. Still, don't limit yourself by thinking you can only hang with the girls you cheer with, are on your soccer team, the drama club kids, or the mathletes. **Shake it up** by getting to know people with different personalities, opinions, and interests. So seek out five fresh potential pals. Even if you just toss out a smile and a "hi," it's a start (that shy new girl in homeroom looks like she could use a welcome mat). You'll wonder why you didn't chat 'em up before.

## ☆ Ease Your Way to That "A"

Most teachers use the first day to get you familiar with how class is going to be run, right? Well, if you go all Nancy Drew and read the clues, you'll see that she's telling you how to get that A by letting you know what she expects. If you follow to the letter the *good-student guidelines* Teach lays out, there's an excellent chance you'll push yourself into A-plus territory. So when she says she hates lates and gives five pop quizzes each quarter, etch that into your brain.

## ☆ Speak Up

You're sitting in English, and Mr. Norbit is going over the reading list for the semester. Trouble is, he's going so lightning-fast you're totally confused about which title's which. When he asks if anybody has questions, though, you clam up—the last thing you wanna do is look dopey.

Here's our tip: **Unzip those lips!** Asking questions is a sign of intelligence. When you put forth the effort to be inquisitive about a topic, it shows you've been paying attention and want *all the info you can possibly scoop up.* So ask away. Chances are someone else is thinking the same thing and has the same question.

## ☆ Take a Risk

Today, it's all about facing that knee-knockin' fear. Yep, you're gonna do the one thing you prayed all summer long you'd have *the guts to do*. Whether it's asking your crush-from-forever if you can sit at his table in study hall or tossing your hat in the ring for class secretary. If the crush ices you out or you spectacularly lose the election, it's no biggie! There's nothing like sticking your neck out to give you a jolt of can-do confidence, regardless of the outcome.

VOTE!

## 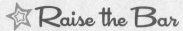 Raise the Bar

Starting today, pick **one tricky thing** to master. Maybe that C you got in math last year has been weighing on you all summer. Why not flip to those tough probs in the back of your new math book and tackle 'em? *Imagine how awesome you'll feel* when you finally get it.

## Share Your Day

How many years have you dragged yourself into the house after the first day and had Mom ambush you with, "Tell me all about it! How were your classes? Are your teachers nice?" Your answer: "It was fine. Nothing to talk about." Mom isn't being all nosy—*she genuinely cares* about your day. So pull up a chair at the kitchen table and share the excitement.

# Going From Public to Private School?

**Some of you may be making two transitions: Not only are ya headed to middle school, but it's a private one, too. Don't fret! It's going to be different than your public school, but here's what you need to know.**

☀ **Smaller Classes.** You'll get more one-on-one attention from your teachers because the class sizes will be significantly smaller. This means extra attention in the classes you may struggle with and more challenging assignments in the classes in which you excel.

☀ **Uniforms.** You won't have to worry about what to wear every day because most private schools require that you sport a uniform.

☀ **Parental Involvement.** Because your parents are paying money for you to attend this school, they may be more emotionally invested in your homework and grades.

# Success in School

You've heard that you get insane amounts of homework and tests in middle school. There are stories about one teacher who tests students without warning, and another who assigns, like, ten hours of homework a week. Ten hours?! You can't even imagine how you're going to get through the first week, let alone the first quarter!

*RELAX!* We've got good news for ya: Most of these rumors are probably just *false bits of info* passed down to you from sneaky upperclassmen. OK, so maybe you will have a lot more homework and the teachers will expect a lot more from you now that you're in middle school. But it's all just to prep you for what lies ahead in high school and then college—and it will definitely be doable. Just think of all those who did it before you!

## HANDLING A WHOA! WORKLOAD

So here's the deal with middle school: You're going to have at least six subjects with a different teacher each day. Some of those teachers may love piling on the homework while others can't wait to surprise you with a pop quiz to make sure you're paying attention. And some may give you no homework but expect you to look alive and participate during class. You may have papers to write or group projects to plan over several weeks—and that's just in the first semester.

**Sounds scary, huh?**

But as impossible as this whopper of a workload seems, we promise you that it'll be more than manageable. You just need to approach your academics in a, uh, smart way. So get started!

# TIMING IS EVERYTHING

Never before has time management been so mega-important in your life. Planning ahead, spacing out assignments, and making the most of every hour in your day will keep you from flipping out at super-stressful times (like finals week or the night before a huge deadline). Plus, you'll be able to sail right through the semester with great grades to show for it. Of course, becoming a master of time management isn't such a cinch. It takes, um, time—and plenty of practice. But we're confident in you, chica. **Especially if you try these tips:**

 ## Don't Wait

Your teacher assigned a report on *The Great Gatsby* at the beginning of the semester and you've yet to crack the book—you've still got a week, right? Not a masterful move. Instead, get the ball rolling on an assignment as soon as you can with short stints of work, starting with fifteen- to thirty-minute periods. Write a quick rough outline, doing the intro one day, followed by the first couple of paragraphs the next. Breaking up the big projects will make everything seem more doable—and cause much less stress for you. After all, it's easier to be motivated when you're not freaked out by an overwhelming amount of work.

## ❁ Time It Right ❁

Energy gives you the ability to do work, so try doing most of your tasks when you have the most of it. Everyone's internal clock is different, so figure out when you're the sharpest. You're an efficient early bird? Memorize those lines while eating your Cheerios instead of going through the motions while half asleep at night. Or use the momentum of a post-school day buzz to crank through flash cards or practice your English speech once you get home.

## ❁ Squeeze in Work ❁ Whenever You Can

Another way to maximize every minute? Take advantage of things like study hall to get work done. Bang out vocabulary sentences fifteen minutes before volleyball practice starts. And, divide your lunchtime in half: First part for gossiping with your girls and the second part to catch up on your chapters.

# ✿ Keep the Focus ✿

Even if you have the best intentions to get an early start, motivation can melt when you're dealing with distractions. So eliminate potential pitfalls by shutting down AIM and turning off your cell and TV while you work.

But know that it's okay to take a break—especially if you're not accomplishing anything and your concentration is crumbling. Grab some water or a nonsugary snack, stand up and do ten jumping jacks to get your blood moving, or try some deep breathing exercises.

# ✿ Be Balanced ✿

Finally figured out how to get things done ahead of time? Keep up the momentum by staying organized: Use a planner and fill it up with future tasks to tackle over the next few weeks. Just make sure to leave some free time, too—letting yourself have a little fun will only make you more serious about studying. Try to make work and play tops on your to-dos, and you'll get that extra push to succeed.

# BEAT TEST STRESS

*So you're committed to working hard and ahead of time.* Fab! At least you've got your homework under control. But then there are those pesky things called tests you've got to deal with on top of everything else. It's just a fact of life that you're going to have to accept: Quizzes, midterms, finals, and major tests are all part of your education post-elementary school. Many may even account for major parts of your grade, so it's not like you can sleep through 'em.

*So, how to train your brain to triumph over tests?* Well, first there's that whole studying sitch to deal with. As we warned before, saving studying 'til the last sec will only sink you like a stone on test day. Instead, plan to prep for two weeks 'til test time for thirty minutes to an hour a day. That way, you can gradually learn the information.

*Your final exam will likely focus on key concepts,* so max out your energy on the material your teacher has gone over the most. Once you know those things inside and out, rewind to the background stuff, like less important dates, little-known names, reeeeeally short Civil War battles. . . .

**And the night before the test?** Reinforce the work you've put in by reading through the material one last time. Then slam those books shut and relax—listen to soothing tunes, play with your pooch, take a yummy vanilla bubble bath. Hit the sack early—studies show a good night's sleep helps you remember what you read once the A.M. rolls around.

**Then, during the test, keep your nerves in check by carefully reading each question.** When you feel sure about an answer, give yourself an inner shoutout—think, "Amazing" or "Got it!" If you find yourself choking on a question, don't trip up—breathe steadily until it comes to you. Completely stumped? Move on, and go back to it later if there's time. Speaking of . . . avoid too much clock-watching.

**Finally, for many girls, taking a test isn't half as scary as waiting to get it back with a grade.** What happens now is out of your hands, so throw yourself into decorating the gym for the dance or doing drills on the field. Stay busy, and you might even forget about it, at least until Teach starts handing back those papers. The thing is, you're gonna take tons of tests in your lifetime, and you'll handle each and every exam with increased skill and self-assurance. We give you an A+ for choosing to handle the heat this time with super self-confidence.

# Cram Like a Champ

Once again finding yourself just a few days away from that monstrous math test? We'll spare you the lecture on planning ahead again and instead give you the goods on cramming wisely with five foolproof steps to sweet last-minute studying success.

## Break It Up

Compact your cram time into two-hour blocks: Crack the books from seven to nine P.M. each night leading up to the exam (any more will sap your sleep—not good for a busy girl like you). Then, dedicate a portion of your weekend to the books, again cramming in two-hour blocks with one- to two-hour breaks in between.

## Be a Speedy Reader

When it comes to browsing those books, read the intro to each chapter, skim the first few sentences of all following paragraphs, then skip ahead to the last page for a nice summary of the points covered throughout. Doing this saves time while giving you a good grip on the key concepts that'll most likely land on your exam.

## Master Memorization

Storing a semester's worth of facts and figures in your noggin is no easy task. But tricks like making up an easy-to-recall song (replace the lyrics of your fave tune with key terms or phrases) or saying dates and facts aloud will make the content more relevant to your world—and help your brain recall it later on.

##  Study Right

Study on your own for at least a few hours until you've got the pivotal points down, then gather the girls for a big review the night before the exam. Drill each other on key concepts, compare and share notes, and hash out the harder stuff so you're all clear on the content.

## ✳ Quit While You're Ahead

When you're feeling serious brain pain, simply stop working. Power down the laptop, take a bubble bath, have a healthy snack (try almonds, which are natural memory boosters), and get some shut-eye. Going into an exam anxious and fidgety will just distract you and crush your concentration.

## TRY THIS! BURST THAT BUBBLE

Studying for a major test? Instead of munching M&M's, start blowing bubbles. A recent study found chewing gum reduces stress and anxiety. Plus, the motion gets blood flowing, which'll help increase memory and concentration.

*So get chompin' and watch those scores soar!*

# Super Study Tips!

**Here are some quick hints to help you stay calm, cool, collected, and organized all year round!**

## Take a break

Research shows that regular breaks and fun boost grades. Use these play times to release and unwind when you really need to de-frazzle.

## Squeeze it in

oeuf (egg)

Make flash cards on index cards before important tests, and have them handy in between classes or in the carpool lane. Stuck in the waiting room at a doctor's appointment? Whip out your binder, and review your week's notes. Brainstorm ideas at the bus stop about special projects coming up, and jot them down.

## Lighten up

A change of study space or routine might be just what you need to get motivated. If you usually study with bright lights, tone it down with indirect light (make sure you're not straining your eyes). If you use the dim-light approach, try a switch to some bright fluorescent lights. Rain, snow, wind, or shine, studying by a big window may also improve your grades by giving you the boost of energy you need.

# DON'T CHEAT YOURSELF

**A big reason** you may be tempted to cheat is being unprepared for a test or having trouble remembering dates and facts. Lazy study habits are other big reasons as is pressure from your friends and other classmates. And, many girls cheat out of desperation. Whether you can't make time around soccer practice or are being plain lazy, sometimes you just don't study well enough for an important test. Top that off with your folks vowing to cut off online privileges if you don't get decent grades, and the pressure is on full blast.

**Tina, twelve, is a good student** but found herself in a pinch. She had missed a few days of school to go on a family vacation, and Tina's teachers had given her work to keep up while she was away. But her first day back to school was a killer. "The day was fine until math," Tina explains. "We were handed an assignment, and I didn't understand it. It was something different than what the teacher had told me to study. I couldn't go up and ask her because it was my reputation to be 'the smart one.' Then, I just looked over at my friend's paper and copied. I am sorry I did it because now I don't understand how to do that math formula."

Like Tina, many girls who cheat feel they have only cheated themselves of what they were supposed to learn from the assignment.

● ● ● ● ● ●

**Even though few girls** get caught cheating, most realize the consequences. Perhaps this is because the handful who do get caught in the act set an example for the others. Polly, twelve, cheated twice without incident, but the third time her teacher found out:

"I had to call my mom and admit it and ask her what my punishment should be. I was so embarrassed."

● ● ● ● ● ●

**Sonja, eleven, didn't get caught,** but learned that cheating has other potential pitfalls. "I looked at the paper of the girl across from me," she says. "It turned out she had the wrong answers anyway."

# THE TEACHER TRIALS

With all of those tests and papers they're tossin' your way, it may seem like your teachers are totally tryin' to ruin your life. But no matter how hard they are on ya, we swear they're not out to get you—or ruin your report card. Most likely, the tougher the teacher, the more confidence they have in you to get everything done. (They might just have a weird way of showing it.)

Still, the road to pleasing your teacher may be a bumpy one—especially when you're just starting out middle school and don't really know what to make of 'em. So to stop your teachers from squashing your slammin' school vibe, here are some insta-ways to impress them.

## HOW TO BRING UP BAD GRADES BEFORE IT'S TOO LATE

⊚ *Need a break?* We'd like to hope you won't have to ask for many when it comes to your grades. But let's face it: Middle school is tough, and it's perfectly natural to go through ups and downs (and by that we mean going up to an A, then all the way down to a C and back up again). The cool part about grades is that they're fixable for the most part—if you address any problem areas the second you start to feel stressed.

⊚ *First step?* Let's circle back to the importance of having a good (or at least decent) relationship with your teacher. He or she is

35

your best ally when your grades are slipping and likely will do everything to help give you a boost.

**"I just did not get pre-algebra at all,"** Emma, thirteen, remembers. "I was struggling, but because I went to my teacher every step of the way, she raised my grade because she saw that I was trying." Just remember that your teacher will appreciate your initiative and take it into consideration when handing in final grades.

*If studying when your grades are slipping* just seems like a daunting task, recruit a bud to join you in your grade-boosting adventure. You can compare class notes, study together, and encourage one another. Foolin' around on Facebook instead of studying for your math exam? Log off that laptop and call your study buddy. Tell her to come over—pronto!—to work on equations. You can fire off

QUIE
Study
Hall

facts out loud and explain the super-tough stuff to each other.

**Or maybe you need absolute silence.** Try studying at the library, where it's super-quiet. In class, try taking the seat right in front. It may not be so exciting sitting all the way up front, but you'll be less tempted to turn around and talk to your friends, or doze off and start drooling.

 *You could also try to find soothing music* to play while you are studying. We wouldn't recommend trying to study while blasting your favorite tunes (you'll be totally tempted to start singing along). But maybe some classical music or smooth ocean sounds will do. Really it's up to you to find what works best.

 *If these tactics don't work, talk to your parents.* They may be able to get you a tutor to help pull your grades up. If nothing helps, you might want to see a doctor or counselor. You could have a condition such as ADHD (attention deficit hyperactivity disorder), which may explain your short attention span. So, if you think your prob is serious and none of these solutions work, see a doc!

# HOWDY, PARTNER!

**Once you hit middle school,** you'll quickly discover that teachers love assigning projects that call for you to work with a partner. It sounds fun, but beware—there's a lot more to stay on top of and a lot more responsibility that comes when working in groups or with a partner.

**For starters, you have to be open-minded** when it comes to who is in your group. Chances are, you're not gonna have a say, and your teacher knows better than to pair you up with your best friend. Get over it. Look at your group project as an excellent life lesson in working out of your comfort zone or as a fab new chance to make some new pals.

**Elissa, thirteen, was freaked** out when she was put in a semester-long group project with three kids she always thought were not very friendly and pretty snobby. "I ended up really getting along with them," she remembers. "In fact, we totally started hanging out after the project was over, and I became really close friends with them all."

**So, when you meet up** with your group members for the first time, clearly divvy up and write down everyone's responsibilities. If it's all in writing, no one can ever say they didn't know what was expected of them later on. Next step is to get out a calendar and map out firm dates for when each part of your project needs to be completed. Even if you have three months to get it done, your group should get on a schedule so you're not scrambling the weekend before it's due.

**"Having a calendar was a lifesaver** in a group project I had in English class that was worth half my grade," Kara, fifteen, remembers. "When one of the members tried to insist that he had no idea what day his part was due, we just pointed to the calendar and there was no argument."

**Another way to gain group project bliss?** Communicate as much as possible. You all need to stay in touch in between deadlines to troubleshoot or even share new ideas or brainstorms. Set up regular online chats or even create a Facebook group for your project where you can share information and regularly stay connected. If you're having trouble with the things you're responsible for working on, you must let your partners know immediately. Everyone in the group gets the same grade and you don't want to be the one whose poor work made the difference between an A or a B!

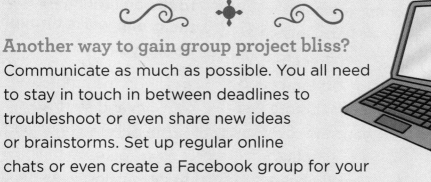

# QUIZ: WHAT'S YOUR SECRET LEARNING STYLE?

Are you a show-me student or more of a listen-and-learn kind of gal? Knowing how your brain works best is the new, easy way to an A!

**1. Your fam's heading to Paris—how do you plan to perfect your language skills in time for the trip?**

A) Create an online slide show with pics—and the pronunciations—of popular Parisian sights.

B) Download French-language podcasts and listen to 'em before bed.

C) Have your BFF over once a week to practice *parlez-ing Français*.

D) Rent French flicks (no subtitles!) and check out foreign newspapers and fashion mags at the library to teach yourself.

**2.** Dad's driving ya to a new bud's house for a sleepover. How do you direct him there?

A) With landmarks.

B) Call her for instructions, then repeat 'em to Pops.

C) Find her street on a map and navigate with point-to-point directions.

D) Just wing it.

**3. Your class is taking a trip to the aquarium. As soon as the group walks through the doors, you . . .**

A) Hit up the amphibian room and start reading the bulleted facts and stats on each tank.

B) Listen closely as the tour guide talks about the exotic fish.

C) Scope out the hands-on tank. You can't wait to pet a stingray!

D) Ignore the tour and roam the building solo.

**4.** You're giving a presentation on the Irish Potato Famine in history. To prep, you . . .

A) Write down your speech over and over to help you memorize it.

B) Record yourself giving the speech, then play it back 'til you get all of the important facts and dates.

C) Do a full dress rehearsal with your parents as the audience.

D) Review your notes the night before, then just go for it.

**5.** You just spotted an old friend whom you haven't seen in ages. The first thing that jumps to your mind about her is . . .

A) That cute mini dress she wore to the sixth-grade farewell dance.

B) Her high-pitched voice and contagious laugh.

C) The dance you both choreographed for the first-grade talent show.

D) Um, not much. Her name is Brooke, right? Or Blake?

## MOSTLY A's • *The Eyes Have It*

You absorb everything visually, so you can't quite grasp a concept unless you actually see it. So during lectures, take astute notes and draw diagrams and charts so you really get the picture. And if you blank on a question at test time? Close your eyes and visualize where that info was on your outline—it'll come back to you.

## MOSTLY B's • *All Ears*

You learn through listening, and you need to listen to get everything Teach is tellin' ya. Don't be afraid to ask her to repeat anything you may have missed, and read your notes aloud so all of the info sticks.

## MOSTLY C's • *All About Actions*

You learn through experience, so try sparking up the sedentary stuff by volunteering to read chapters out loud or to lead a class demo. Then, give your brain breaks by studying in short chunks of time and keep moving—you'll concentrate better.

## MOSTLY D's • *Self-Taught Student*

You learn through experimentation, so it's best to set up a list of goals, then come up with your own ideas on how to make 'em happen. Since you work best on your own, study for exams solo. Try creating practice quizzes, and flip through flash cards each night before bed.

# THE BOTTOM LINE . . .

No doubt, school's gonna be stressful. But it's nothing—we repeat *nothing*—you can't conquer. When things get hectic, just keep your spirits up with positive chatter. Tell yourself that yes, you'll definitely get that work done. Yes, you can score an A on that English exam. Yes, you can make the honor roll. Whatever your mantra, just make sure you're stickin' to it instead of letting school beat you up or make you feel stupid or lame. Because you know what? You're smarter than that!

# If at First You Don't Succeed...

Sometimes, no matter how much you study, or how many times you talk to your teacher after class, things still may not go your way. Maybe you won't be able to bump that B up to an A or you'll get a lower-than-expected grade on a paper you could've sworn was a masterpiece. That's just life for ya. Sure, it stinks to accept a bad grade. It's even worse having to tell your parents about it. But it doesn't mean you're a failure. At all.

We all are bound to bomb a test or perform under par once in a while, so when it happens to you, don't  beat yourself up. Instead, find the lesson you can take away from the experience—whether it's switching up your study habits or adjusting your writing to mesh with your teacher's style. Figuring out whatever it takes to do better next time will be an effort well worthy of an A!

# Shining Outside the Classroom

**S**o, now you have all the knowledge you need to study smart, ace those exams, and handle a killer course load like a pro. No doubt you're going to be working super hard this year, so we hope you give yourself some time to play, too. Yep, you're allowed to have fun at school—in fact, it's encouraged!

And by fun, of course, all of those extracurrics you get to choose from in middle school are included. From book club to band to basketball, most middle schools offer tons of activities. And joining one (or two or three) *will make ya more well-rounded* and give you the chance to do something you love while having a blast.

Then again, each extracurricular can eat into the time you've set aside for other important stuff, like studying. Because with all of these opportunities comes the possibility of taking on too much. **You must make sure you can handle your homework** along with helping the homeless, planning the fall dance, or whatever it is you choose to do after school. But as we told ya before, it's all about managing your time and knowing how to scale back when you've piled too much on your plate.

*And how to go about doing that?* Read on, busy babe. We're here to clue ya in on clubs and sports—plus offer some ways to make every aspect of middle school mesh.

# GO AHEAD, JUMP RIGHT IN

So you've made the commitment to join a club. Great! But how to choose one when there are so many amazing extracurrics to pick from?

Maybe you want to start your very own fashion line. Or perhaps you wanna perfect your Spanish skills. Most likely, there's a club that'll match your interests and give you a chance to spend time doing something you really love. Of course, when you're interested in everything from saving the Earth to sewing, it's hard to decide in which direction to head.

But try to narrow it down to three that you are the most excited about joining. Then find out everything you can about them—when they meet, membership requirements, minimum time commitment—and pick the one that makes the most sense with your schedule.

# QUIZ: WHAT'S THE BEST ACTIVITY FOR YOU TO JOIN?

So many clubs, teams, organizations and activities, so little time! If you can't figure out what to join first, take this mini-quiz to pinpoint what club is the best fit for you!

**1.** In your spare time, you would rather:

A) Shoot hoops with the neighborhood boys.
B) Recycle cans you find strewn around the neighborhood.
C) Browse Barnes & Noble for hours on end.
D) Organize your closet and desk drawers—and then head over to your best friend's house to do the same for her.

**2.** You're flipping through the channels and you stop on:

A) A cheerleading competition on ESPN.
B) A PBS documentary on endangered animals.
C) *The Soup* on E!
D) Whatever is on CNN.

**3.** The celebrity you most identify with is:

A) The Williams' sisters—both Venus and Serena are stars in your world!
B) Miley Cyrus
C) Tyra Banks
D) Hillary Clinton

**4.** Your favorite subject is:

A) Gym
B) Social studies
C) English
D) American history

**5.** Your friends call you first when they:

A) Need to know who's going to the Super Bowl.
B) Find a stray animal.
C) Need a recap of the latest issue of *US Weekly*.
D) Want a list of possible candidates who will run against Obama in 2012.

**6.** The word that best describes you is:

A) Competitive
B) Compassionate
C) Energetic
D) Organized

**7.** The main reason you want to join a club is to:

A) Make new buds who share the same interests.
B) Make an impact in your community by volunteering.
C) Follow your deepest passions.
D) Get a head start boosting up your resume for those college applications.

## MOSTLY A's • *Sports Team*

You have school spirit and are a true team player. Take that energy and go try out for whatever makes you happy, from track to cheerleading.

## MOSTLY B's • *Eco Awareness*

You want to change the world and have big plans to fix the things wrong on Planet Earth. Find the groups at school that want to help the environment.

## MOSTLY C's • *Newspaper/Yearbook*

You want to know everything going on at your school, from who's dating who to why everyone's outraged over the cafeteria lunch menu. Joining the newspaper or yearbook staff is the perfect way to put on your reporter hat and be the one in your group who's completely in the know.

## MOSTLY D's • *Student Government*

You're a born leader and love standing up for what's right and wrong. Joining student government gives you the opportunity to be the voice for your fellow classmates while making sure things at school are being done fair and square.

# THE FRIEND FACTOR

And as you're making your decisions on a club, please **do not factor in what your friends are joining.** Sure, if you're all crazy about cooking and want to join the **Top Chef Club** together, then by all means go for it. But if your sights are set on something else, then you should simply follow your heart.

• • • • • • • • • • • • • • • • • • • • • • • • • • • • •

**Colleen, twelve, was devastated** that she was the only one of her friends who even wanted to join a club. "I was bummed that my friends from elementary school were too scared to try something new," she remembers. "I joined the dance club anyway and it was the best thing I ever did. I made new friends, kept in shape, and never had any regrets like I know my other friends did by not joining." And don't worry, your pals will understand.

• • • • • • • • • • • • • • • • • • • • • • • • • • • • •

And if you're starting something solo? **Good for you!** Clubs are awesome ways to bond with new buds. Everyone's in the same boat, so ya shouldn't stress about being a stranger. All you gotta do is walk into that first meeting with an open mind and use your shared interest for that sport or activity to create some common ground for an initial convo.

**Tryin' out for a team can be an awesome addition to your middle school experience.** You'll meet new friends, and playing sports is great for you. Even if you've never kicked a soccer ball or laced up a running shoe, you could end up being totally awesome at your sport. And if you're not so hot in the beginning, we bet the girls who are vets will def be happy to help you out—after all, sports are a team effort!

# Get Sporty

**Still, it's understandable if you're freaking a bit** about acing that tennis tryout or making the cut for cheerleading. Tryin' out for a school sport can be super intimidating, even if you're properly prepped (i.e. you've been practicing your soccer header all summer).

**But when it comes to showing your stuff,** try not to take things so seriously.

**Let your skills speak for themselves** and show you're an all-around team player: Arrive early, offer to help carry equipment, and don't get super down on yourself if you make a mistake. A girl has to know how to recover to be a great player. And remember, it's only a game!

# Get Prepped for Sports Tryouts

## ⭐ Eat extra healthy

Being hydrated is key in any sport, so chug water like crazy. Sticking to healthy snacks like granola bars, fruits, and veggies will help your body stay fueled.

## ⭐ Stay prepped

Make sure that you bring everything you need. There are always physical forms and permission slips, so to be on your coach's good side, bring the paperwork on the first day. And don't forget a water bottle and all the necessary equipment. There's nothing worse than getting sidelined for leaving your gear at home.

## ⭐ Get pumped!

Make a playlist of your all-time favorite upbeat music. Listen to it before tryouts to get your mind and body pumpin'. While you do this, remember back to one of the best games you ever had, and visualize yourself scoring the winning goal or throwing the fastest pitch. This will keep you positive and ready to go!

## ⭐ Rest up

Going to bed early is key. It will seem impossible because of the nerves, but do something that makes you tired like reading or watching TV, and then hit the sack. That way, you will be completely refreshed and ready to play.

# Avoiding Overload

**So you chose a club** or selected a sport and now your sched's stacked like a plate of pancakes at IHOP. You're a busy babe and it seems like you've barely had time to breathe let alone finish those chapters or write up that report. So, how can ya make your middle school sched work without going completely crazed?

**First up, you gotta focus** on the important stuff—like schoolwork—first.

**Save things** like pedicures and TiVo catch-ups for Saturday, and tackle tasks with a definite deadline. If you can't seem to get organized, set reminders on a Google calendar and highlight ultra-busy days in your planner. Prioritizing—not procrastinating—will make your must-dos more manageable.

And make sure you don't take all your activities so seriously. A little bit of LOL can go a very long way. Studies show a sense of humor can relieve stress and lead to success. So if your first day of dishwashing in the soup kitchen leaves you covered head-to-toe in soapy water, laugh it off and go with the, um, flow.

And if ya get in too deep? Don't panic! You can slowly scale back and select a couple causes close to your heart, saying oh-so-sorry to the rest. Say you're all about fundraising for charity, but not into cooking. Then volunteer for that 5K for leukemia, but pass on the band's bake sale. That way, you'll be able to give what you're really into your all—and stay sane while you're at it.

Connie, thirteen, can relate. "I wanted to join everything. I couldn't believe how many great clubs and opportunities my school had," she remembers. "But then, my grades started to slip and I had to drop out of a few clubs and let the members down when I couldn't finish projects I had started for them."

The last thing you want is to start off middle school with a bad reputation for joining everything—but then following through on nada. Try to remember, a club you don't have time for this year may slide into your schedule next year, so you don't always have to rush into everything right away.

# Real Girls Weigh On:

## Why extracurrics are awesome

☀ "The drama club changed my life. I was cast in our spring play and became such good friends with the entire cast and crew—I even met my first boyfriend there." —Morgan, 15

☀ "I made a difference in my community. I joined an after-school mentoring program, and the young girl I tutored told me I inspired her not to do drugs and cut class like her siblings before her did." —Faith, 13

☀ "It boosted my GPA. A lot of my teachers were also advisers to the clubs I was a part of. They got to know me better and so I felt more comfortable going to them if I was struggling with their assignments." —Alyssa, 14

☀ "Writing for my school newspaper helped me land a summer gig at the local paper. They needed help a few days a week and were so impressed by the writing samples I had to show them that they hired me on the spot." —Meg, 16

☀ "Being involved in clubs helped me get my homework done faster. I'd be motivated to get work done in between classes or at lunch so I could enjoy my meetings rather than stress over the work I was going to have to do when I got home late." —Samantha, 13

# Running for Office

So let's say you found a club that you're completely psyched about. You're totally involved in everything they do and have yet to miss a meeting. You have a million ideas for ways to make things better and know exactly how you'd go about making those changes. Sound familiar? Then you may want to think about stepping into a leadership role, like club president or a student government officer.

Taking on an office is a *ginormous* responsibility—and will require a ton of extra hours on your part. But besides a great GPA, nothing impresses teachers more than an involved student. Plus, you'll get a perfect chance to get noticed at school and really make your mark.

Lila, thirteen, loved being in student government because of all the great things they did for her school, like putting on a big school dance and fundraising to paint the girls' locker room. When she took on the office of secretary, she noticed that it really affected all areas of her life. "People listened to what I had to say in meetings so it really boosted my confidence," she said. "I would sometimes let my friends walk all over me before, but being a leader in student government helped me gain the confidence to stand up for myself."

**Of course,** it's not like you can slide into that secretary seat in a snap. Most likely, you'll have to be elected as an officer, which means ya gotta impress your classmates with a killer campaign.

**So as you're working** to snag their vote, make sure they know all the reasons why they should check your name on that ballot. It's not enough to promise "awesome changes." You have to point out specific issues you'll tackle and lay that all out in your campaign. Pick things you know are important and possible to achieve: Raising money for after-school activities is perfect. Getting a heated pool? Not so much. If you choose unrealistic goals, students will be bummed when you don't pull through.

**An important note:** Even if you're super-anxious and nervous on the inside about the outcome of this election,

keep up a cool and composed exterior. Don't badger or beg people to vote for you, no matter how neck-and-neck you are with your opponent. Remind yourself that this determines whether you're elected to office, but it doesn't outline your life achievements.

**And if you're elected?** Congrats, girl! You deserve it! After all your hard work, you're bound to do a brilliant job. Just stick to what you promised, listen to your classmates, and do what you can for them and your club. But if you didn't get the gig, don't ditch your dreams when there's a bit of a setback. When things don't go according to plan, give yourself a little wallow time, and pursue your passion another way. So you didn't get elected to student gov. So what? You may not be the prez, but you're still gonna shine. And don't forget—there's always next year!

# THE BOTTOM LINE . . .

Sure, it may be a struggle at times to keep all of your classes and extracurrics in check, but remember that this kind of non-stop schedule is getting you prepped for the rigors of high school, college, and even your career. And while being a well-rounded gal is important, so is your sanity! So if you feel like you've taken on too much, scale back. Even your passions can become pains when you don't have time for 'em.

# Changes in Your Crew

4

It's hard—no, impossible—to imagine school sans your buds, right? But for some of you, the switch to middle school may mean you've gotta leave your crew behind. Maybe one of your girls is going to private school and another is heading to the magnet program across town. Some of you will go to school with your besties but then have completely opposite schedules. *Whatever the reason, there may be a chance* that you and your girls are splittin' up—and it's really sad to think about.

But here's your shining, silver lining: Middle school is a place where *new friendships form every day.* So while you may miss mingling with your BFFs on the playground, you'll have your pick of potential pals. Of course, that means you'll also have to deal with drama like blending the old buds with the new crew. But that's what we're here for!

## ❁ MOVING DAY

Let's say your fam just moved to a new neighborhood and you're starting school solo. Scary, huh? You have every right to panic—after all, you've been side-by-side with your crew since kindergarten. But as tough as it may seem to tackle a new crop of classes and fit in among all of those strange faces on your own, it's actually not so bad. Really.

# No Fear!

**First off,** give people a chance. Try sitting with different groups at lunch every day. Do you and the girl from art class love the same music? Join her in the caf on Tuesday. Need help with your math homework? Ask the class brainiac if he/she wants to grab a bite. After a while, you're sure to find a few friends you like and maybe even a BFF.

**And don't forget** to get involved. Join a sport or activity, or maybe give volunteering a try. By getting involved, you have something worthwhile to do—and you'll get a mega confidence boost and some new pals with similar interests while you're at it.

**Take it from Alex, fifteen,** who danced her way to friendships when she started at a new middle school. "I almost didn't take ballet after I moved because I didn't know if everyone would be better than me," says Alex. "But my mom convinced me it didn't matter, so I decided to try. I got to know one girl pretty well, and it turned out she was in my class when school started. We hit it off and she then introduced me to a lot of other girls in our class."

**And as you start** meeting and mingling with new mates? Try opening up a bit. If you feel good chilling with them after school, start handing 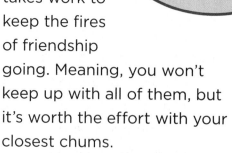 out your e-mail, phone number, or AIM screen name. The more time you spend with people, the more comfortable you will feel being the honest-to-goodness you. So, why not have a gab sesh with the goalie after field hockey practice instead of heading straight home like you usually do? Taking a few extra steps (and some extra minutes in your day) to make an effort will steer you in the right direction when it comes to making more friends.

**And when you're meeting those new buds,** it's tempting to compare everything and everyone to your tried 'n' true pals. This, my friend, is a bad idea. How would you like it if a new friend kept comparing you to her old friend?

**And no matter what ya do**—don't forget your old friends. Because as much as you tell each other that you'll K.I.T. no matter what (that's "keep in touch," btw)—it takes work to keep the fires of friendship going. Meaning, you won't keep up with all of them, but it's worth the effort with your closest chums.

# DEALING WITH THE DRAMA

Let's say your BFF is suddenly inseparable with the most popular chica in school and their incessant inside jokes make you feel totally left out. Or maybe you made the cheer squad and your girl didn't—and now she refuses to even look your way on game day.

*Sometimes, though, it's not that easy to head in different directions drama-free.*

Though it's normal to go through ups and downs with your BFF during middle school, it still hurts. But there are ways to try to salvage your sisterhood—or at least make life a little easier on ya. *First off, don't just ignore the prob.* Try talking to her in a tone that's honest and straightforward as opposed to accusatory (calling her names or blasting her for being a bad friend are definite don'ts!).

*No matter what, hear her out:* Maybe she's just excited to have new friends and can't see that she's making you miserable.

And if the void remains after your chat? Well, your bud bond may have veered, but that doesn't mean it has to come to a permanent halt. Figure out what you and your girl can still agree on. *Make an effort to spend low-key time together.*

# Surviving Separation Nation . . .

So you and your BFF can't get your class schedules to sync, but you want to keep your friendship going strong? Here are four tips to stay tight.

## 1. Get clubby

Find clubs both of you are into, and hit the sign-up sheet! Extracurriculars add up to extra friendship time.

## 2. Noteworthy

Let your friend know you think of her by sneaking friendly notes into her binders when she's not looking. Slipping an occasional card in her locker is nice, too, and don't forget to text during lunch (if you're allowed).

## 3. Book it

Hit the stationery store and pick out a funky notebook the two of you can share. Take turns writing and doodling in the book, trading it off when you see each other.

## 4. Weekend warriors

Live it up on the weekends. Keep each other updated on funny stories from class, awesome (or not so awesome) teachers, the cute guy who sits next to you in history, and new friends you two should hang out with. And, of course, make some oh-so-fabulous memories together, girl!

# MAKING NEW FRIENDS

Whether your bud's branching out or you're just hoping to make some different friends on your own, middle school's a great time for adding new folks to your life. And how to do that, exactly? Well, we've all heard about being friendly and open, but what follows are the less obvious tips for making new friends. (We're talking way beyond Facebook here.)

who will watch hours of cheesy reality TV without judgment."

## 🌸 Mix it up 🌸

Don't think you've gotta stick to one crew or one type of pal. It's great to have a mix of buds, especially if you have tons of different interests. You can have some people as "friends," some as "good friends," and some as "best friends." You can also have "math class friends," "youth group friends," even a "friend

## 🌸 Get perky 🌸

Think about the last time you were in a really killer mood, like right after you aced a test or scored the winning goal. Remember how you felt like you could do anything, talk to anybody, and it didn't matter if the cutest guy in school said hi back or not? Try to project a bit of that infectious spirit into every day.

Yes, some days are hard enough to get through without trying to be perky on top of it. But new people notice a good mood and like to surround themselves with people who are positive—that's how life goes. While you don't want to be totally fake (no one expects you to crack jokes if your hamster just died), you do want to put your best face forward.

##  Learn to read

No, not Shakespeare—body language. By watching people's faces, expressions, posture, and body movements, you can tell how they are reacting to and perceiving you. You probably already have some experience picking up subtle clues. If your mom slams the door on her way in and smacks the grocery bags on the counter, chances are it isn't the right time to ask if you can have a friend over for dinner. That's body language.

But often, when we try to make a good impression, we focus so much on what we are saying and doing that we forget about the person we're trying to impress in the first place! Smiles are an easy way to tell if someone is into you. Take a moment every few minutes to check out the facial expressions of the person you're chatting with. Is she giving you her rapt attention? Or looking down the hall?

And while you have to start a friendship somewhere (talking about the weather counts), try not to make too much out of first encounters. Every once in a while, you'll instantly hit it off with someone, but most people will be a bit reserved until they get to know you better. Respect their distance, and keep things quick and light for a while.

## Avoid over sharing

It's hard to resist the temptation to spend every waking moment with a new friend. You want to share everything with her. But some people feel overwhelmed by so much instant attention, so don't Krazy Glue yourself to her.

**Plus, remember you had a life** before them. Keep up with old friends, practice your flute, write a screenplay, whatever. If you are desperate to be friends with someone, that person will pick up those vibes. Let's face it, no one wants to hang out with someone who comes off as being really needy.

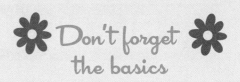

## Don't forget the basics

Have something to talk about, be it the latest movie or what you did over the weekend. Be supportive when someone needs it. Be a good student (no one wants to hang out with troublemakers—detention is not a fun activity to share). Really listen to what other people are saying, and resist the temptation to hog the spotlight (even if you think you have a million great stories to tell). And finally— yep, we'll say it—be yourself. Because even if you're great at pretending to be someone else, people can see fakers from a million miles away. Plus, why work so hard at being someone you're not when you're so effortlessly fabulous!

# BLENDING BUDS

So you've met a few super-cool pals and now you want to introduce them to your group. No doubt, your new friends will be awesome additions to your already amazing crew, but the key is to ease everyone into the transition. First, check with both sides to make sure they're open to meeting. Chances are, they'll be into it. But asking before introducing shows you're taking their feelings into consideration—not just yours.

*Since crowds can be intimidating,* introduce the newbies to two current chums at a time. That'll give everyone the chance to get to know each other. Do something simple like an impromptu trip to the mall or stroll to DQ for sundaes. Keep it short, make it sweet, and let the bonding begin!

**When you do bring all of your buds together,** some of your old friends may stick together out of habit instead of reaching out to the new girls. To make sure no one's left out, start up casual convos that everyone can chime in on, like thoughts on last night's hot TV show or new movie. Fight the urge to make inside jokes, as they're bound to leave a newcomer feeling clueless.

**Once all the intros have been made,** kick-start the school year—and new friendships—by inviting everyone over for a BBQ. Compare notes on who has the hardest class, dish on your teachers, confess crushes on the new cuties. Giving your girls another opportunity to bond outside of school will really help seal the deal.

**Now, with all that said, you can't force friendships.** So if your attempts to blend buds backfire, don't feel like you have to now pick one pal over another. It's totally cool to have a few crews of friends to hang with.

# THE FIVE PALS YOU GOTTA HAVE

These are the five types of pals you've gotta have in your circle from morning announcements until the dismissal bell rings....

## 1. The "Head Cheerleader"

When you feel less than motivated, she's the go-to gal for a tender lovin' shove in the let's-get-it-done direction. Why? She has loads of energy and an infinitely sunny outlook on life.

## 2. The Study Buddy

She's not necessarily the smartest girl in your grade, but she's right up there in conscientiousness. She knows what's due when, and she'll save you a seat in the library if you want to join her for a study sesh.

## 3. The Gossip Girl

Don't confuse the gossip guru for a rumor monger—that's not her game! She's never mean-spirited, and she refuses to pass on false info. And you can always count on her to be in-the-know. This girl has the juice on everything in and around school grounds. Drink it up.

## 4. The Guidance Counselor

Look to your no-nonsense pal to put your problems into perspective for you. She's rational, low-key, and keeps everything top secret. Best of all? Her advice is solid.

## 5. The Role Model

She excels at what's important to you . . . and you hope she'll pass the torch. So tune in to how she crops an image or sticks a dismount. Let her pave the way for you to join her on the pedestal!

# The Dos and Don'ts of the Friend Blend

☀ **DON'T** introduce all the girls at once.

☀ **DO** mention to the new and old crews how cool it would be if they met. Showing up with an outsider—unannounced—might come off like a sneak attack.

☀ **DON'T** be upset if two girls you think are a match made in heaven turn out to be a royal disaster.

☀ **DO** think about which new bud is the most outgoing and wouldn't be intimidated by a new group. Then invite her along next time you hit the mall with the old gang.

☀ **DON'T** try to force a friendship. If a new and old friend don't hit it off, let it be. You can't expect people to gel if they're just not feelin' it.

☀ **DO** be patient, and let the awkwardness wear off before determining whether or not a match is successful.

☀ **DON'T** forget the most important rule of friendship: Treat all your friends with respect. You know, the way you want to be treated.

BFF

# YOUR MOST BURNING BFF Q'S—ANSWERED!

**"MY BFF IS PRETTIER,** SMARTER, MORE TALENTED, MORE FUN, AND HAS A BETTER PERSONALITY THAN ME. EVERYTHING IS SO EASY FOR HER—HER LIFE IS PERFECT WITHOUT ANY EFFORT AT ALL! I STILL WANT TO LIKE MY FRIEND, BUT SOMETIMES IT'S LIKE I FEEL WORSE WHEN I'M WITH HER. WHAT SHOULD I DO?"'

Your BFF's seemingly perfect life is not without effort. She faces the same everyday challenges as you and everyone else, but the difference is how she deals with them. Next time you're around your friend, take note of her attitude. Is she always looking at the bright side of things? This may be why people are drawn to her. An upbeat, friendly personality is an awesome trait to have, so toss aside your grumbling, jealous mood and put a smile on! Stop comparing yourself to your bestie and begin embracing yourself for you. You're different from her and everybody else in this world, so shine on!

**"I HAVE TWO FRIENDS** WHO FIGHT CONSTANTLY. THEY BOTH WANT ME TO TAKE THEIR SIDE. THEY THREATEN TO NOT BE MY FRIEND ANYMORE OR TO NEVER TALK TO ME AGAIN. I'M STUCK IN THE MIDDLE OF ALL THEIR FIGHTS, AND IT DOESN'T SEEM FAIR!"

**No matter what happens,** DON'T take sides. Listen to each side of the story and try to mediate any conflict as objectively and calmly as you can. Suggest ways that the girls can deal with their problems without favoring one over the other. Then tell both of your friends individually that it hurts your feelings tremendously to be shoved in the middle. Use "I feel" statements to tell them that you care about them, but that you don't want to take any sides. You want the best for your friends, so tell them to deal with their drama by themselves.

**"IT'S ALWAYS BEEN HARD** FOR ME TO GET GUY FRIENDS. I DON'T PLAY SPORTS BECAUSE I'M REALLY SHY AND SELF-CONSCIOUS. HOW DO I GET A BGF?"

News flash, girlie: Guy pals are everywhere . . . you just gotta go out and talk to 'em! If you LOVE to read, go to the library. You can always strike up a convo with a guy that you see in the sci-fi section (your fave!) or any boy in the check out line. Love saving the planet? See if your school has an environmental club (coed, of course!) where you can meet eco-conscious boy buds.

## "MY FRIEND LIES A LOT TO ME. LIKE A LOT, A LOT. I WANT TO BE HER BFF, BUT I HATE IT WHEN SHE LIES AND KEEPS SECRETS FROM ME. SHOULD I STAY FRIENDS WITH HER?"

**Your bud's lying may** actually be a cry for help. Are there serious issues going on at her home that may explain her unusual behavior? Is she having fights with her parents? Are her siblings driving her insane? There may be tons of reasons for her actions. But the only way you're going to find out the truth is if you ask her. It's important for you to ask her in a respectful way. If you walk up to her and call her crazy she'll probably never speak to you again. But if you let her know you're concerned about her and you've noticed she's been acting differently lately, she may be a lot more willing to talk.

## THE BOTTOM LINE . . .

Some friends are forever (like your BFF, duh!). But others may be part of your world for much less time. Truth is, your taste in friends is always changing, kinda like your taste in clothes and guys. So if a friendship fades or you and your once-chummy chica just aren't clicking anymore, it's okay. Just let things end naturally without sparking any unnecessary drama by, say, starting a fight or doing something else intentionally icky. You never know when you may meet up again!

# All About Boys

**L**et's face it: Middle school really isn't just about tough teachers, homework, tests, and extracurrics. Yes, we're talking about boys.

Of course, most have had boys in class since pre-school but, up until now, many of 'em were either *your worst enemies or annoying pests* who picked on you in gym class. Then, one morning, boom! Is it just you or is brace-face Brendan—the one who used to bring a SpongeBob lunch box to school every day—now a hottie soccer player with to-die-for dimples?

See what we mean? **Guys add a whole new element** to your life now that you're noticing them in a different way. And, before you know it, you'll have your first serious crush (if ya haven't already), maybe even your first real BF. So to clue you in on everything you need to know about guys, here's a chapter *dedicated to understanding* all those cuties in your class (and making your relationships with them rock!).

# INSIDE THE MINDS OF MIDDLE-SCHOOL GUYS

Think you know guys like the back of your manicured hand? Think again! For all girls, it sometimes feels like it'd be easier to score a 2400 on your SATs than to determine what's really going on inside a boy's brain. But instead of spending one more second tryin' to figure out why they do what they do, just keep reading.

## HOW DO I KNOW IF HE'S INTO ME?

**Listen up, girl:** He's not just saying you look cute in that dress for the heck of it. A boy is generally a pretty easy book to read. If he's digging you, he'll let you know with some blatant behavior like going out of his way to talk to you and giving you lots of long stares each time you pass him in the hallway. Phone calls, text messages, or some Facebook or AIM chat time means he wants to connect with you and get to know you better because he's interested in finding out about what makes you tick. If during one of those calls you mention you're struggling in biology and the next day he slips his notes in your locker? Uh, yeah, he's not just being a nice guy . . . he's being a nice guy who wants to make sure you know he is into you.

# BUT DOES HE LIKE ME . . . OR LIKE-LIKE ME?

**Sure, you and your crush** may spend tons of time together and IM all night long. But before you express your interest, look for clues that his interest may be purely platonic: Does he have a bunch of girl friends (two words) on speed dial? Is he always talking about how hot the chick in his bio class is? Is he really flirting or just being extra-friendly? If you know what to look for, it may become painfully obvious that the two of you are on the fast track

to Friendship City. If that's the case, hop off the love train before your heart is run over and re-route your affection toward a different crush.

## ARE WE—OR AREN'T WE?

**You may be waiting** for that moment when your guy stares lovingly into your eyes and asks if you'll be his GF. Newsflash: This will probably never happen. Most boys aren't crazy about lovey-dovey chitchat and don't see the need for such formalities. But if you're dying to know if he's ready to take things to that next step, simply sit him down and ask him. Don't make a big deal of it—a casual, "So, is it okay if I call you my boyfriend?" over pizza will do. You'll get your answer and he'll be touched. Seeing your new status confirmed online may be fine, but nothing beats hearing it straight from your sweetie.

# IS HE OVER ME?

**Among all of the things** guys are good at (making you melt with one smile; looking hot in basketball uniforms), expressing emotions may not be one of 'em. Guys can be downright devious when it comes to serving up the awful truth. And instead of being honest with you about their fading feelings, some prefer to push you away.

Your guy may be uncomfy with confrontation, but that doesn't mean you have to put up with this awful act. As soon as you sense he's losing interest (he's all over you one minute and practically ignoring you the next), call him on it. Ask him over after school for a chat to see what's up. If he's willing to work things out, great! But if he continues to ice ya out, move on—and read on (we have tonsa tips for doing just that later in this chapter!).

# THE 411 ON flirting

So now that we've taught ya a little bit about what's going on *inside the minds of those boys,* you gotta be able to engage 'em with your fantastic flirting skills. Surprise, surprise—boys are shy, too, and the only way they're going to keep things going is **if they know you're digging them.** *Flirting* is the only way they're gonna get that message loud and clear. Sure, you may think it's enough to sweetly smile without stopping when you pass your crush in the hallway, but subtlety is so not top on the list of guy strengths, and *your coyness may be misinterpreted as a lack of interest entirely.* So, next time you really want to let a guy know you're interested, try out these no-fail flirting tips.

## Don't wait for your crush

It may not be the "traditional" thing to do, but **guys definitely dig when girls make the first move.** Believe us, it's better than their clumsy attempts to break the ice with goofy opening lines and other botched attempts to impress you. By approaching a guy with a simple, "What's up?" or "Did you download that iPhone app?" you'll save him the stress of coming up with a cheesy opener.

## Get sporty

Want an insta-way to wow a guy? *Stock up on your sports knowledge* (or whatever else he's into). And take advantage of any chance to **get in the game**, be it going one-on-one on the b-ball court or challenging him to a Call of Duty 4 duel. Don't have the sporty skills? Don't worry, it's not about winning. **Think of it as your flirting security blanket.** You'll feel more confident knowing that you know something about the stuff he's into (and it'll show!).

## ✽ Charm him

Sure, a cute dress can snag attention, but what you're wearing will only get 'em to glance your way—it's your personality that'll get a guy to **hang on for the long haul.** Honestly. So sit down at a table full of guys in the caf and get involved in a paper football game. If you're at a party, don't huddle in the corner with your crew—put yourself out there in the middle of things and let the guys know that you're in the room. Laugh at their jokes, tell some of your own. **Whatever you can do to show off your sparkling personality** will eventually captivate them with your charm.

## ✽ Chat right

*Of course, flirting isn't just about face-to-face encounters.* Both guys and girls spend every spare second communicating via computer or cell, so naturally, you flirt this way, too. When it comes to chatting with girls online, guys don't want to beat around the bush with idle small talk. Keep the convo flowing with funny banter (not one to bust out the quips? Links to hilarious YouTube clips show you've got a sense of humor).

Finally, try being a little aloof—being the first to say good-bye or sign off will leave him longing for more.

Gotta go!

Flirting is *a gateway to another point in a relationship.* So details definitely matter. Yes, you may be getting lost in their baby blues, but guys like when you pay attention to what they have to say. So listen to them, then follow up on something you learned during the convo. If he mentioned a big test or tryouts, send a text or e-mail wishing him luck. After all, a little ego boost never hurt anyone, right?

Of course, relationships are not one-way streets, so check that the guy is *paying as much attention to you as you are to him.* If that's not the case, all of your spectacular flirting is probably best focused elsewhere. That's not to say you should give up if a guy doesn't go for these moves right away. Just relax, be yourself, and hope for the best.

# Your Best Flirting Secrets

☀ **Fabulous flattery.** "Most guys love nice words as much as we do. My crush and I are both band geeks, and I complimented his awesome marimba solo. I could tell he was pleased to hear that!" —Abby J.

☀ **Make contact.** "To get a guy's attention, I just kind of gently bump into him and say 'Oh, sorry, my bad.'" —Anna D.

☀ **Do the tap dance.** "If you've talked at least once, it's always cute to tap him on the shoulder as you walk by. Keep walking, and when he turns to see who tapped him on the shoulder, no one will be there! When he turns to look the other way, he'll see you tapped him on the shoulder. Smile and wave, but keep walking. Stay chill. My crush always blushes when I do this." —Emma B.

☀ **Start the convo.** "You have to get to know a guy before you get him to like you. I usually crack jokes about school or the lame party we're at. Very rarely do guys like a girl they don't even know!"— Sarah S.

☀ **Laugh.** "If he sees you aren't too serious, he'll feel more comfortable with you. Would you want to be with someone who never laughs?" —Alexandra B.

☀ **Be yourself.** "The single most important thing is to be you, because chances are, he'll see through it if you aren't. Besides, it's so much easier and more fun to be you anyway! If he doesn't get that, then he isn't as awesome as you thought." —Hayley D.

# OMG, He Likes You!

## You did it!

You flirted like a pro and you and that cutie of yours are officially an item. You can't stop replaying in your mind the moment he asked you out (though you gotta try 'cause your schoolwork can't suffer) because it was just perfect. Having a guy to call your own is one of the best parts of getting older, but relationships take a lot of work. So things stay as sweet as when you exchanged your first smiles, we have the tricks of the trade to keep you and your guy all aglow.

● ● ● ● ● ●

### Be each other's No. 1 fan

You know how you and your best friend always have each other's backs? Well, you and your guy should do that, too. Whether it's giving him a pep talk before his big bio test or him screaming his head off at your soccer game, the more support you can give each other, the tighter of a twosome you'll be.

Also key? Being honest when one of you has done something that isn't so cool—you don't want to just

acknowledge the good stuff or keep your feelings bottled up inside. The worst is exploding because you didn't speak up when you should have. But the bottom line is that you're both in this relationship because you think pretty highly of each other, so make a point of showing it!

## Keep some things private

Sure, it's super fun to dish with your friends about all of the cute things your BF does for you. But when it comes to revealing all about your relationship, try to keep some things sacred. No one needs to know everything that goes on between you and your guy. Keeping some things just between the two of you is one of the best parts of being in a relationship—besides, your BF likely doesn't want you airing all of his laundry to anyone

who'll listen. So, next time your girls press ya for those personal deets, fill 'em in on what's going on with you and your honey, but save some of the more personal stories for just the two of you.

## Embrace imperfections

You shouldn't be afraid to goof off or slip up every once in a while, and neither should your guy. Getting to know your BF's quirks—whether it's burping, sloppiness, or nonstop sports blabber—is part of getting to know him. You should always call him

85

out if he does something that hurts or offends you, but you can't expect him to be Mr. Perfect all of the time—how boring would that be? Plus, if you cut him a little slack, he'll be way more understanding next time you have a whoops moment, like when you're running twenty minutes late to meet him.

## Get in with his buds

You may invite your guy everywhere, from tagging along with your girls to the mall to study sessions, and he goes without a complaint. So when he wants you to come to a Guitar Hero night at his bud's house, it's a no-brainer for you to go and get to know his crew. Guys are very loyal to their other guy friends. It's just an unwritten code. So you should show up with your guy the next time he invites you to hang with his buds 'cause it's a big deal.

Get to know them, let them tell you funny (and embarrassing) stories about your guy, and just let them see all the great things about you that made your guy ask you out in the first place. With that said, you don't want to cling to your guy in front of them and act like his security guard. If his crew feels like you're dictating who your guy talks to and how much fun he can have, you're going to lose points with them—and your guy—fast!

### Have fun

Whether it's shooting hoops, playing Wii Fit, or hanging out and watching old movies, having some one-on-one fun will boost your bond. And if you don't have that one thing you both love doing together? Try out an activity that's new to both of you: Sign up for photography classes or join the tech crew for the fall play. That way, you'll get plenty of hang-time—and undoubtedly be able to share some hilarious moments.

# Never Been Kissed?

## WELL, FIRST THINGS FIRST:

If you're not ready to take your relationship to a more physical level, don't. The right guy will understand if all you can handle right now is holding hands and flirtatious smiles. Don't panic if you are ready but have never had the opportunity to kiss a guy—yet. Everything happens for everyone at a different pace. You can't compare what your friends have done to your own experiences. Just relax and take comfort in knowing that good things happen to those who wait!

# QUIZ: ARE YOU BOY CRAZY?

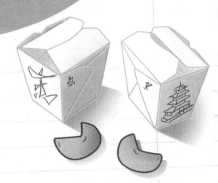

Would your friends say you're sane and rational until the topic of B-O-Y-S comes up? Take this quiz and we'll be the judge of that!

1. **What best describes the decor of your bedroom:**

A) Pictures of friends and family, and a bulletin board with important notes and mementos.

B) Just one pic of Chace Crawford by the bed, but otherwise lots of framed artwork picked up on your last family vacay.

C) An absolute shrine to every hot celebrity. Robert Pattinson? Check! Zac Efron? Check! Jonas Brothers? Check . . .

2. **You're at a slumber party with your BFFs. The first thing you do is . . .**

A) Decide if you're ordering pizza or Chinese for dinner.

B) Rank the hottest boys in school.

C) Plot a foolproof strategy with your pals to get your crush to ask you out.

3. **You'd only bail on your planned hangout with your crew if . . .**

A) Your parents majorly guilted you into participating in family fun night.

B) You were grounded for staying on the phone with your crush past curfew.

C) You locked eyes with your crush earlier in the day and are now holding out for his call. Because he's so calling, right?

**4. Your latest issue of *Girls' Life* has arrived in the mail. You immediately flip to:**

A) The BFF section.
B) The cover story on your fave celeb.
C) Anything and everything with the word "guy" in it.

**5. How many guys would you say you've crushed on in the first half of the year?**

A) There is just one name on the list because you can only focus on one guy at a time.
B) At least five.
C) Way too many to count.

## Answers

### MOSTLY A's • Boy Sane

You like boys as much as anyone, but keep things in check. You know there's more to life than just obsessing over guys, so you have a great balance going on.

### MOSTLY B's • Boy Nutty

You have boys on the brain, but in a healthy way that doesn't drive your friends and family crazy. You know how to reel it in, but you still like to think about your latest crush whenever you get a minute!

### MOSTLY C's • Boy Fanatic

You have three things on your mind 24/7 and they are boys, boys, and more boys. Whether it's your latest crush, the cutie you pass every day at lunch, or your slew of celeb loves like the Jonas Brothers, guys are always front and center in your brain. You might want to find another hobby—there is more to life than guys and you don't want your friends and fam to get sick of your nonstop guy-centric chatter!

# WHEN TO KISS YOUR GUY GOOD-BYE

SO NOW THAT WE'VE DISCUSSED THE OH-SO-MANY REASONS HAVING A BF CAN BE AWESOME, WE'VE GOTTA TOSS A SLICE OF REALITY YOUR WAY: Relationships aren't always so wonderful. Boys will be boys, and well, unfortunately some are bound to be bad for you. They'll cheat, ignore your texts, leave ya hanging in the hallway, or—gasp!—leave ya for someone else. Or sometimes, your BF isn't even a bad guy—he's just bad for you. So how to know when it's time to say buh-bye to your guy? Look for these telltale signs.

## You're just not that into him.

Your BF clearly adores you: He hangs on your every word, surprises you with sweet treats, texts you constantly just to say, "I miss u!" Only prob? You don't quite have the same feelings for him. And though the constant flattery can be nice, it can also get overwhelming when you're not, well, sharing the love. So spare your sensitive sweetie any future heartache by halting things now. He'll find another girl to gush over, and you'll have the freedom to find someone who really makes you melt.

## You're with him for the wrong reasons.

It's not easy being the lone single girl in your group of friends, or the only one who's never had a boyfriend. But settling for a guy who's less than stellar is not a good enough reason to enter coupledom. While you may be able to say, "I have a boyfriend!", if your heart's not in it, why waste your time and energy? So evaluate your relationship and figure out if it's really worth it. If not, break things off and take pride in your single status.

## ❋ You're too busy for a BF.

This week, you've got tennis practice, singing lessons, and a babysitting gig. Top that with family obligations and BFF time and you're left with mere minutes to spend with your guy. As much as you'd like to make things work, the reality is you just aren't at a place where a BF is a priority. And that's totally OK. There will be a right time for a guy—it's just not today. Or this year, even. So tell your BF that you just can't commit to a serious relationship right now. He'll understand. And if it's really meant to be, the two of you can try again when you've got a less-crammed calendar.

## ❋ You're out of his league.

Slinging insults at underclassmen reeks of silly playground nonsense that was never actually amusing at all. So if your BF's bordering on immature, realize you can do better. In a few years, maybe he'll be worth another date. But for right now, let him keep kidding around while you find a grown-up guy you really groove with.

## ✱ You're bored.

Another Friday, another Netflix night with your BF. Yawn. While you used to be OK with the low-key hangouts, these days you're totally bored by your boy. Before you give up on your guy, suggest you do something different on your next date (bowling, a hike, a bike ride—whatever will spice things up). If he doesn't budge—or you still find yourself thinking about doing anything but spending time with your sweetie, take that as a major sign that it's time to turn this guy loose.

## ✱ You're crushing on other guys.

OK, it's not like you have to turn off your cute guy radar. (Hello! As if ignoring the hotties in the halls is even an option.) But if you are wishing and hoping that the math genius in your fifth-period algebra class will finally put two and two together and realize you are, uh, "four" him, it's time to bid your current fella farewell. Even though you really do like him, it's not really fair, is it? So say, "Let's just be friends" (in a nice way!), and mean it. That way, you can keep crushing without worry.

# Letting him down— the nice way

When you've caught his eye but you're still looking the other way, here are two quick ways to say no—nicely.

*Give it time*. You never have to give immediate answers. You have every right to say you aren't sure. Here's a way to do it: "I'm flattered that you asked; I'll get back to you." If he's cool, he'll accept that without pushing. If not, you don't want to be with him anyway.

*Be direct*. There isn't really a way to decline and not hurt his feelings. The kindest way to say it is plain and simple: "I really appreciate your asking me, but I'd rather stay friends." You're done.

## Handling Heartache

Try as you might to avoid it, breakups are bound to happen. Whether you are the dumper or the dumpee, it's gonna hurt, but it is possible to get over a broken heart. Promise! Here's how . . .

### Throw a (brief) pity party

Well, we're not gonna lie. The first day of a breakup is a huge, honkin' disaster. It's crucial to get the icky emotions outta your system, and you can't do that without experiencing them. So, for one day only, hustle home from school and dive under the covers. Chow your way through a carton of ice cream. Call your BFF and talk about how wrecked you feel. Now, bawl yourself to sleep.

## Figure it out

Once the shock wears off, you're gonna feel mixed up about why you were dumped. Was it something you said or did? Don't blame yourself! To stop agonizing over every doubt-filled detail, write down five things you didn't like about dating him. Maybe he sneered at your jokes or eyeballed other girls. Instead of dwelling on what you could have done differently, be way honest about his faults and shortcomings.

## Pamper yourself

There's nothing like a bad bust-up to cause a girl to forget how gorge she is. Reality check: You are completely foxy. To get back in touch with your hotness, tell your BFF to bring her makeup case to your casa first thing after school. Then, spend the afternoon enjoying a full-on makeover. Let your girl spruce up your 'do, polish your nails, gloss up your lips, and totally babe you out.

## Get back out there

When your BF stopped diggin' your gravy, you were convinced no other guy would ever be into you, right? It's normal to feel this way, but stop it! Go to that party tonight and talk to at least three guys. No rebounding—just focus on some nice convos so you'll see that boys really are still into you. There will be tons of dating fun in your future.

# GUYS TO AVOID

We know it's easy to be swept away by a guy. But some of them are best kept far from BF status. Here's a look at some of the bad boys you'd be wise to avoid.

## ☑ 24/7 BOY

24/7 monopolizes your time and needs to be the center of your universe. He has a freaky way of trying to make you feel guilty when you're not with him. You deserve to have a life outside of this relationship. If he makes that difficult, it's time to let him go.

## ☑ USER LOSER BOY

He's sweet as powdered sugar—when he's getting something out of the deal. This guy looks out for one person and one person only—himself! Since he's so busy making sure it's all good for No. 1, you'll be lucky if he even considers you No. 2—especially if your dad gets rid of those Giants tickets.

## ☑ UNCOMMON DENOMINATOR BOY

He's a funny e-mailer. But on the phone or in person, you have zip to talk about. What's wrong with this guy? Honestly? Probably nothing. But, he's wrong for you! A great smile and witty e-mails do not a relationship make.

## ☑ MAKEOVER BOY

He thinks you would look better if your chestnut locks were blond. But it's not just that: He has something to say about everything you say, wear, or do. His "constructive criticism" can be a self-confidence killer. It makes him feel important, but you don't need someone who wants to turn you into someone you're not.

## ☑ HOUDINI BOY

One day you have a blast together, the next he's MIA. This guy will never remember your middle name or birthday, even if you give him multiple choices. If his now-he's-here/now-he's-not stunts are becoming a predictable pattern, sorry, but it's time to make Mr. Inconsiderate disappear for good!

# Fitting In and Stressing Less

So maybe it's not the older students or the really huge school that's making you freak about middle school. Nope, what's got you crazy is your concern about fitting in.

Whether you like to rock a different style, are super shy, or just step to your own beat, *it's always tough to mix in with the masses.* And being on the outside looking in is not so fun. But guess what? You're going to find a place where you feel completely comfy—with friends and with yourself—it just may not happen on day one. But to speed things up in that department, **here's more on feeling right at home** (and as happy as can be!) in school.

# 🌸 FINDING YOUR OWN NICHE

*News flash:* **The average teen has just four to six good friends. Yep, less than you can count on two hands. That should make you feel better about not being BFFs with your entire class! And while it's fun to see your Facebook friend count go up, when it comes to honest-to-goodness buds, quality is much more important than quantity.**

**With all of the stresses and pressure you face every day, *it's no shocker* that a whopping sixty-two percent of girls ages eight to seventeen feel insecure or not sure of themselves.**

**But as scary as this statistic is, there are** plenty of quick and simple ways to help you feel good about yourself.

## Be Your Body's BFF

**You know how sometimes you look in the mirror and just don't like what you see starin' back?** Whether it's a ginormous zit on your forehead or the way your jeans feel tight in all the wrong places, we all have those bad-body days. But that doesn't mean you should hide under a hat or in baggy clothes for the rest of the school year.

Instead, **find whatever it is you do like about your body and show it off.** Sure, you may have a zit—but check out how that new skirt shows off your muscular legs! As you flaunt your fab features—and rack up the compliments—you'll forget all about those so-called flaws. **And remember, you are so much more than how you look.**

## Be Proud

**That big ol' brain of yours is stored with all sorts of info.** So why keep all of that knowledge to yourself? Be proud to share your smarts in school: Impress your class with your fierce French accent, wow 'em with your powerful poetry, and raise your hand to answer Teach's tricky chem Q. **As long as you're not a super show off about your straight-A attitude,** there's no need to keep your skills under wraps.

## Be a Good Friend

**You know how you always turn to your best bud when you have a problem?** Maybe it's the way she listens to your every word or lets you obsess over your crush for hours and hours. Whatever it is that makes your pal perfect, make sure that you are showing her the same love. Ask what's going on in her world. **Offer words of support when you know she needs a pick-me-up.**

Simple, sweet acts will put a gigantic smile on her face—and make you feel great. After all, even if you think your relationship's already pretty solid, **really being there for your other half will make you feel more whole.**

## Be a Do-Gooder

It sounds cliché, but reaching out to those who are less fortunate really does make you feel better about yourself. **So get hooked on helping:** Raise funds for your fave cause, visit with an elderly neighbor, tutor a classmate, or go snuggle with puppies at your local pound. Whatever you choose to do, **you'll be amazed at how helping others can instantly lift your spirits** and give you a sense of purpose.

## Be Passionate

Upping your self-esteem can be as simple as stepping out of your comfort zone and trying something new. Love photography? Register for a summer session at the community college. Nuts for knitting? Check out group classes at a nearby sewing shop. Doing something you're actually passionate about will send your confidence soaring—and everyone will flock to you.

## Be Yourself

So maybe you don't have that one dress that everyone will be sporting this season. So what? If you're spending your time comparing yourself to others, well, **you're wasting a lot of precious minutes.** Especially when it comes to pricey material possessions—what's in one second will be out the next, so why bother buying it in the first place?

**And whether it's your eclectic taste in tunes** or your funky fashion or your awesomely out-there sense of humor, be happy with whatever makes you you. After all, you're one of a kind, babe. Don't ever forget it!

# KISSING SHY GOOD-BYE

## ✿ Check Yourself

Slouchin' down? Got your arms permanently locked across your chest? Feel safer staring at the floor tiles than making eye contact with your new locker partner? **You've probably heard this before,** but people truly do pick up on closed-up (literally) cues like these.

So before you cruise into school that first day, do this quick check: **Take a deep breath to calm yourself, then hold that head up high,** let your arms swing freely by your sides and, **most important, smile!** No matter how nervous you feel inside, you'll appear to be cool and confident to others. Who doesn't want to meet someone like that?

## ✿ Talk It Up

Sure, it's easy to wait around for someone to strike up a conversation with you, but sooner or later, **you've gotta learn to initiate** some interaction.

Think you don't have the gift of gab? No fear, future Chatty Cathy, we've got a plan. **The trick is to start small** by saying hello to one new person every day of the first week.

Your next move after they say hey back? Spark convo by feeding off your common ground. See what a girl from your homeroom thinks of your wacky teacher. Ask the guy who sits next to you in class a question like, "How long did it take you to finish last night's assignment?" Then all you need to do is smile and listen.

**Compliments work, too.** Give props to someone's new bag or cool tee. Even a simple move like swapping your go-to spot in the back of the room for a desk up front (those are usually the ones picked by the most outgoing gals) can connect you with a classmate.

**The bottom line?** Treat every social encounter as if you have nothing to lose. Because guess what? You don't.

 Don't Give Up

You know that old saying "fake it 'til you make it"? It's truer than you think. So after you get through these first weeks, keep working on strutting your stuff, saying hello, kicking off convos, and gettin' involved.

Besides, the things that keep us from putting ourselves out there are almost always unnoticed by others anyway. Does your face get red when you talk to a new guy? He'll just think it's because the AC isn't cranked enough. Don't like speaking up in class because of your squeaky voice? Our bet is people consider it cute. But even if they don't, should you care? Nope. Why? Because it's part of you. And that's good enough.

# POP THAT PRESSURE

**Pressure—it's everywhere. Whether you're putting it on yourself or your teachers or parents are piling it on, it probably feels like you're walking around with a 150-pound weight on your shoulders these days. It's hard to stay excited about your experience in middle school when, instead of catching zzz's, you find yourself wide awake, frettin' and sweatin' over every last detail that could sabotage this school year right out of the gate.**

What if you trip on the bus and fall on your face right in front of the homeroom hottie? What if you don't get any classes with your BFF? What if your locker is thirty million miles away from civilization? What if every single dumb little thing that could possibly go wrong actually does go wrong, and your school year is cursed from day one?

First things first. You need to know that *you've got the power to make middle school totally awesome.* It's time to stop torturing yourself with confidence-zapping, brain-draining worries. Yes, it's utterly natural to brood over certain major issues in life. **Lots of times, though, everyday worries get blown way out of proportion.**

The trick is to put what's dogging you into the proper perspective. *Stomp out the anxiety so you can solve stuff straight-up.* Letting go of worry means letting go of stress. **Worrying can make you feel insecure,** irritable—and weirdly in control of the sitch. This is because when you sit and stew about something you can't do anything about, you trick yourself into feeling like you're doing something about it.

*One thing you absolutely cannot control is how other people behave.* You have no power over what that mean chick in your gym class says about your volleyball serve. What you can control is how you react to what she says about you. If it isn't true, ya just gotta let it roll.

*With worrying comes pressure—they go hand in hand.* When you put pressure on yourself to be perfect, you're probably about ready to blow a gasket. Yeah, not really an awesome way to live your life. Pop out of yourself for a minute and consider this: If your BFF were worrying herself sick over school, what would you tell her? That she's only human, right? **OK, so be your own BFF!**

# ZAP STRESS RIGHT NOW

A recent study found that nearly half of teen girls report feeling frequent stress. But that doesn't mean you should let stress sink your middle school experience. This can be your best year ever. The key? Try these proven stress-busters:

## ✳ BE REASONABLE

Fab plans are great, but are your goals realistic? **You don't have to be extraordinary to be successful.** No one is a perfect student, musician, friend, artist, dancer, or athlete. Limit after-school stuff to a few activities, and commit to only one sport each season.

If you find that your sched is way too stacked, it's probably time to scale back. **The best thing to do is slow down and take a break.** Then, focus on your talents and strengths, whatever they are. Concentrate on the things you really dig and you'll be too happy to even think about stress.

## ✳ STAY BALANCED

Girls who feel content usually have mastered a balance of work, play, and rest. Sure, there are lots of things you'd rather be doing, but getting your assignments out of the way first is smart. Get behind and you have to play catch-up.

**It's okay to take breaks, too.** Doodle, write poems, play flute (just for fun), listen to CDs, or daydream about your crush. And don't diss the social scene. Hang with friends, gab on the phone, and surf online. Just don't overdo it. Um, balance, remember?

# ✳ THINK POSITIVELY

Self-confidence goes the distance. Think of yourself as a girl who can handle stress well, and it's likely you will handle stress well. Put the kibosh on pointless comparisons to superstar sibs and buds, and just do your own thing.

**As for slipups? Hey, they happen to everyone.** Overreacting will just worsen the stress. When you drop your lunch tray, your BFF makes a rude comment, or you're sporting a head of hair that just won't do the right thing, deal with it. Pick yourself up, and move on. It's just one awful day. Tomorrow, you can start fresh.

# ✳ GAUGE STRESS

Stress can sneak up on you, so try to notice the signs before it spirals out of control. Nodding off in Spanish? Snapping at your sibs? Having another headache? Maybe your teachers are really piling it on, or you've had a cold, a breakup, or more chores to deal with. **Cut back where you can.** Consider turning down the next couple of babysitting gigs or dropping French club for now.

## ✳ BURN IT OFF

Of course exercise is good for your bod. **But a workout can work wonders on your mental health, too.** Vigorous movement, like dancing or sports, lowers tension and increases energy. Not too eager about exercise? All it takes is a quick walk to banish bad feelings.

## ✳ EAT RIGHT

Eating healthy doesn't just do your body good—it can also keep you calm. Specifically, **foods rich in folic acid and vitamin B** (like salmon, brown rice, turkey, chickpeas, and bananas) have a soothing effect on the body, minimizing stress.

## ✳ UNPLUG AND UNWIND

Think you'll just die if you don't text or update your Facebook status every five minutes? Think again. Sometimes **the best thing is to unplug**—you'll come back refreshed.

## ✳ SLEEP MORE

The less you sleep, the more you'll stress. That should be a wake-up call to those who don't get their eight every night. **Try getting up at the same time every day.**

**Even on weekends.** It may feel like a chore to climb out of bed at seven A.M. on a Saturday, but you'll be better off—and less burdened—because of it.

## ✳ *GET HELP*

Many girls hide their anxiety for fear of seeming lame or ticking off the 'rents. But there's no shame in being stressed out. **A truly together girl knows when to ask for help.**

Talk to your parents if you're feeling overworked. Sure, they want you to do well—but they also want you to be healthy and happy, right? Teachers, too, are usually happy to assist. **Get feedback about not only what you are doing wrong, but also about what you are doing right.**

# THE BOTTOM LINE . . .

One day you're feeling like Miss Popular, the next day you're throwing yourself a pity party for one. That's just the way things go in middle school. There will always be stuff in life that's challenging or disappointing. But when you make good choices and keep a cool head, you'll be able to manage things like a pro. And not just in middle school, either—we're talking forever!

# My Best Advice

☀ "I have some advice for girls who are 'different.' **Don't follow the crowd.** I know you've heard it way too much, but it's true. I used to be unpopular because I was different, but then some other people broke away from the crowd, too. So now we're all friends, and we're all pretty popular without sacrificing our personalities. So, like I said, be yourself and hang in there. Decent people can appreciate differences—and who wants mean friends?"

—Alice H., 13

☀ **"Smile! Even when you're feeling down and out,** you'll find that a simple smile will make you and the people around you feel more cheerful. When you smile, other people smile back at you and your brain registers the happy look and starts to work on other happy responses, like easing the tension in your body and calming your heart rate down. So when you start to freeze up, smile away your stress."

—Jamie, 12

☀ "I was hung up on fitting in with the 'cool' group. But their world is filled with drama, and that gets old. **I realized that no matter who you're friends with, they're all cool.** It's just the way you look at them!"

—Grace, 13

# New Year, New You!

For most of you, *middle school* will mark the time in your life when your bod baffles you more than those killer geometry proofs from last night's homework. Ah, puberty. Love it or hate it, we all go through it at some point. There are tons of changes going on, and while your hormones are having a wild party inside your bod, your brain is racing with questions about what's really up with what's going on from head to toe. So where do you find decent answers to those puzzling body Q's? Right here! Here is some insight to your most intimate inquiries.

# YOUR EVER-CHANGING BODY

## I'M STARTING TO GROW BREASTS

### AND IT'S MAKING ME VERY UNCOMFORTABLE. I WANT TO WEAR A BRA, BUT IF I WEAR ONE TO SCHOOL MY FRIENDS WILL BE LIKE, "YOU'RE WEARING A BRA, AREN'T YOU?" WHAT SHOULD I DO?

Middle school is hard enough without fretting about something you have no control over! First of all, never let anyone make you feel ashamed for wearing a bra. Your body is going through changes. What's happening to you is entirely normal, so you should not be ashamed of that. If one of your friends says, "You're wearing a bra!" kindly tell her, "Yes, I am." Your cool, calm, and collected attitude will make it seem like no big deal to wear a bra, because (guess what?) it's actually not a big deal. And don't worry, every girl has breasts. There's nothing wrong with you. Some of your friends will be catching up before ya know it.

## I'M TURNING 13 IN APRIL, AND I DON'T HAVE BREASTS YET. I FEEL LIKE I NEED THEM. HOW CAN I HELP THAT?

**Girl, you're not alone.** This is a totally common concern. If a flat chest is really getting you flustered, you could find a lightly padded bra to make you feel more comfortable. Or you can just strive to accept your body, lack of curves and all. After all, there's some busty gal out there just wishing her chest looked a little more like yours! Take a look at your other female family members. **Genetics plays a big part** in determining when your breasts are going to make their appearance and what cup size you'll eventually have. Asking your mom when she developed her breasts will not only give you some insight, but it may also give you some peace of mind.

## I BREAK OUT ALL THE TIME. EVERY MORNING, I LOOK INTO THE MIRROR AND THINK ABOUT WHAT EVERYONE WILL SAY ABOUT ME WHEN THEY SEE ME AT SCHOOL. WHAT CAN I DO TO GET RID OF MY ACNE?

**Zits happen.** Especially in middle school, thanks to all of those raging hormones. Having a regular cleansing routine can help rid your face of acne, so start by washing your face just twice a day with an acne-formula cleanser. Even though you may feel greasier than normal, too much scrubbing can irritate your skin, leading to even more breakouts. Then, spot treat with benzoyl peroxide. If this doesn't seem to help, see a dermatologist.

**I JUST GREW** AN INCH AND A HALF IN ONE MONTH! I'M ALREADY TALLER THAN ALL OF MY FRIENDS. HOW CAN I DEAL?

**Everyone grows and matures at different times.** Unlike your fellow classmates, you're ahead of the bunch. That doesn't mean you're weird and that doesn't mean there's something wrong either. It's perfectly normal and healthy! Still, it's not always easy being the odd one out. But lucky for you, most of your friends will shoot up in size, too. In the meantime, **try your hardest to focus on the positives.** Have you ever seen a supermodel or pro-athlete under 5' 6"? Have you ever noticed that you never have to get your jeans hemmed, like your shorty pals? That you can always

reach the top shelf? Everyone hits their own stride when it comes to puberty, and you've just been gifted earlier than most of your classmates.

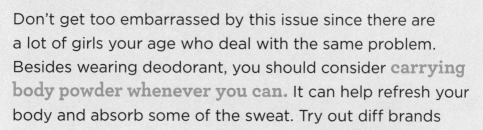

## I HAVE SERIOUS SWEATING PROBLEMS. EVERY TIME I WEAR A LONG SLEEVE SHIRT OR T-SHIRT, I ALWAYS SEE SWEAT MARKS UNDER MY ARMS. IT LOOKS DISGUSTING. WHAT DO I DO?

Don't get too embarrassed by this issue since there are a lot of girls your age who deal with the same problem. Besides wearing deodorant, you should consider **carrying body powder whenever you can.** It can help refresh your body and absorb some of the sweat. Try out diff brands and types of deodorants and antiperspirants to see what works for you. Still sweating? You might want to talk to your parents about it. There are prescription deodorants and cures for sweating that are even stronger than clinical over-the-counter cures. Your doc will also have more tips on how to treat this.

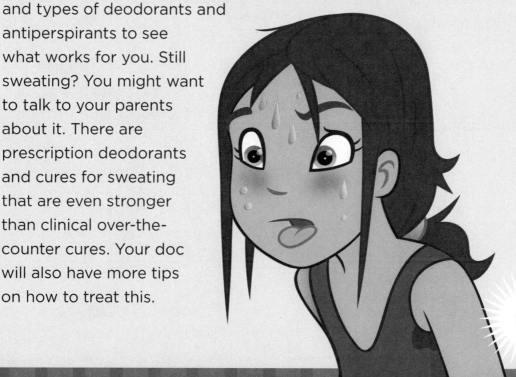

# I HAVE REALLY BAD BACK ACNE!

## WHAT CAN I DO TO GET RID OF IT?

**OMG, as if acne on your face isn't enough,** tons of people (guys and girls) suffer from back acne, or "bacne." Like regular acne, back acne usually occurs around puberty, but it can continue into adulthood, too. But unlike regular acne, stress, oil, and sweat don't seem to be factors that cause back acne.

**To treat mild bacne, wash your back with an anti-bacterial cleanser.** P.S. Unless you're super flexible, you may have to ask your mom or sis to help you out. Then, let your skin dry. After that, apply a small amount of ten percent benzoyl peroxide gel or cream.

If you have really bad back acne, you should definitely schedule an appointment with your dermatologist for a prescription treatment. **To help prevent back acne, try exfoliating at least once a week to remove dead skin cells that build up on your back.**

# 7 steps to LOVING YOUR BOD

Feeling good about your bod makes you more successful at everything you do. So ignore all those weird ideas we all get about women's looks that you see on TV and in magazines. Instead, remind yourself often that you're awesome with these seven steps.

**1. TAKE TIME TO YOURSELF.** Sit by yourself for about five minutes every day. Breathe deeply, and think only good thoughts (no negative self-talk allowed). Taking care of you feels good.

**2. GET STRONG.** Girls who focus more on physical strength than appearance are, in general, happier and healthier.

**3. STAY POSTIVE.** Encourage friends to say only nice things about others' bodies—or tell them to keep their traps shut. Oh, and the same goes for you.

**4. END THE COMPARE-A-THON.** Never compare yourself to others. Ever. Instead, celebrate your strengths every single day.

**5. COMPLIMENT OTHERS.** When someone has a great idea, sunny personality, or major accomplishment, tell her. This helps take the focus away from appearances.

**6. DO RESEARCH.** Understand eating disorders, and be on the lookout for unhealthy behaviors in yourself and friends. For info, check out kidshealth.org/teen and search for eating disorders.

**7. HOLD YOURSELF HIGH.** Adopt good posture—standing tall has a way of making you feel more self-assured.

# BODY AND MIND MAKEOVERS

With so many constant changes occurring in your body, it's perfectly normal to feel more self-conscious during this stage. Maybe you hate your braces or your boy-shape figure. Guess what? Everyone goes through a time when they're unhappy with their body or appearance. The key is to learn to embrace the changes by being comfortable in your own skin.

*First, realize that you are a beautiful girl.* Instead of thinking about what you don't like about your looks, find the things that you've got goin' on! Do you have long, luscious lashes or a killer smile? Focus on your positive traits.

*You can also give yourself a boost by spicing up your look.* Say you've been wearing glasses since second grade. If you've been thinking you'd like to try contacts, ask your mom to set up an appointment with the eye doc.

*Or maybe you've got unruly curls.* Buy a straightener and watch as it transforms your hair! You may realize that curls are just, well, not for you, but a little experimentation is a quick and easy way to pump some energy into your routine. Also, you can rock your look with a little makeup and some new clothes. When it comes to makeup, don't cake it on, girl. Natural is beautiful. Ask your mom to go shopping with you. It will be a special treat for you and will make her feel great 'cause she gets to hang out with you!

● ● ● ● ● ● ● ● ● ● ● ●

*And remember, it really is true that beauty is not skin deep.* So focus on things you can do to better yourself. If you start doing good things, you'll not only become a more mature and well-rounded person, you'll also feel way better about yourself. Join an after-school club or a charity organization that helps those less fortunate. Once you're in do-gooder mode, you'll feel amazing!

● ● ● ● ● ● ● ● ● ● ● ●

*Turn your attention to you* by taking up a self-soothing hobby like yoga, writing in a journal, or dancing. Finding ways to stay busy will help you stress less about how you look. And once you start feeling better mentally and emotionally, you'll look awesome on the outside, too.

Just remember, when it comes to our bodies, we all have the tendency to be our own worst critic. *However, it's necessary to love yourself, no matter what you look like.* These awkward stages are not permanent. Those braces will come off, and those pearly whites will shine through. So go out there and be your beautiful self, girl!

# Eating Right

 *You know that line "your body is a temple"?*

It's totally true! You have to treat it right and, well, worship it. That includes keeping it in shape by working out and eating healthful foods, having a healthy dose of self-confidence, and always listening to your gut. So what can you do to worship that bod?

 *To start, know that you really are what you eat.*

If you want to be energized, alert, and ready to make the most of middle school, you need to incorporate foods into your life that'll get your mind and body at their peak levels of performance. So let's look at your lunch. Sure, it's delish to devour chicken nuggets and fries every day. But as good as they taste, they're not really the best for you. But with some simple swaps, you can have a delish lunch straight outta your (insulated) bag. Here are a few ideas based on classic caf choices:

**BEFORE:**

A serving of spaghetti with meatballs

**AFTER:** DIY antipasto: Cut up lettuce, tomatoes, carrots, onions, lean roast beef, and mozzarella and throw 'em in a container. Drizzle with olive oil and vinegar from the salad bar and pack a whole-wheat roll.

**BEFORE:** A chicken patty on a tasteless, zero-nutrition bun served up with fries

**AFTER:** Slather some leftover grilled chicken in BBQ or buffalo sauce. Cut it up into strips and throw it on a bed of mixed greens. Pile on chopped celery, grated carrot, and a bit of crumbled blue cheese.

**BEFORE:** School pizza

**AFTER:** Spread a whole-wheat pita with hummus, then layer on thin, ripe tomato slices. Now top with pizza faves like green peppers, onions, and mushrooms. Top with grated cheese.

**BEFORE:** Cake for dessert

**AFTER:** Our fave when chocolate's what ya crave? Pudding! Stir in bananas or strawberries! Yum.

# Beauty Tune-Ups

**With five minutes or less to spare, here are some great tips for between classes or on your way to school!**

Apply a light oil-free moisturizer to clean skin (preferably with SPF!).

Lightly brush transparent powder on your face.

Add a sweep of blush to cheeks.

Brush a light eye shadow over your whole lid and brow. Stick to natural-looking soft or shimmery colors—if you mess up, mistakes are hard to see.

Swipe on a stroke of mascara.

Slick lips with a pretty lip gloss.

Do a quick up-do. Just gather it in a ponytail, spin into a bun, and secure with a few pins. When you take it down a little later, you'll have soft waves. Don't worry if it isn't perfect.

Spritz on a subtle scent.

# Shape Up

Once you get going with your middle school routine, you're gonna find that your daily schedule is crammed. *Who has time to work out?* Surprisingly, you do! Believe it or not, a few minutes here and there can add up to a way healthier bod!

*For starters, get going with your workout first thing in the A.M.* by stretching—it'll wake up your body. Reach your fingers to the ceiling, arch your back, and press your feet into the floor—you'll feel your whole body lengthening. Bend over and gently touch your toes a few times. Do a few arm circles. Throw in some neck rolls.

*Of course, sports are a great way to stay in shape.* So if you're on a team, great! But if you're not so sporty, just find something that'll get your heart rate up. Walk, ride your bike, or chase your dog in the snow. And, yes, workout DVD's can be gold-medal material. Just press "play."

# Games that get ya SMARTER!

Umm . . . no you didn't just read that title wrong. *GL*'s got a whole list of games that'll sharpen your test-taking skills. Yep, simple puzzles and even video games with repetitive motions can improve your memory and help you ace that exam. Ready, set . . . **Game Time!**

## Sudoku

This mind-bending numbers game tests your skills while you figure out which numbers fit where on the grid. Try a process of elimination method by getting rid of numbers that don't fit in the empty spots first, and working on what could fit in second. This method totally works during multiple choice tests, too!

## Crossword Puzzles

Crosswords take a ton of pop culture knowledge. They are also great for learning new words and bigger words for terms you already know. Give your new vocab a test drive next time you have an essay or open book test.

## Wii Mario Kart . . . or any Wii game

Twists and turns, breaks, sliding out of the way of oncoming traffic . . . . Mario Kart can be tough! But all those reflexes you sharpen during your Wii game can help you in real life, too. Besides being a bit more agile in phys ed, you can learn to have that pencil out, test ready, and start scribbling answers before your clumsier classmates even have their chairs pulled in.

# FINDING THE TRUE YOU

Your body and looks aren't the only thing morphing during middle school. As you grow up and become more independent, you'll also start discovering who you really are as a person. Nope, we're not talking about whether you're short, tall, curvy, or petite. We mean the non-physical traits that make you stand out from everyone else. But how exactly do you go about discovering who you are?

Do you look for signs in your handwriting, your astrological profile, your palm . . . the soap suds swirling down the shower drain? Instead of focusing inward, look out at what's around you.

Your choices, passions, and preferences define who you are at that moment, so be sure they represent you and not someone else. Don't copy your bestie just

because you think she's great (she is, but so are you!). Don't change yourself to be more like the popular crowd—even if you gain some popular friends, they won't be friends with the real you. Don't be satisfied with always seeing just one type of movie or reading the same kind of novel. Grab a book you wouldn't normally read, try a sport you've never played, or listen to a band you thought you didn't like. **Be open to the possibility of finding new things to love.**

# THE BOTTOM LINE . . .

Finding yourself—and we mean everything from your style to your personality to the things that give you a sense of purpose—doesn't happen overnight. In fact, the exciting journey of finding the true you doesn't end in middle school. It's a lifelong adventure because you are forever changing and growing—yes, even into adulthood. The great thing is, you have the power to be what you want to be—every single step of the way.

You know what makes you shine? Confidence, pure and simple. If you love yourself, love who you're becoming, and don't worry what others think, that's what will attract people to you and make them want to be a part of your fabulous life. Be true to who you are, and be an inspiration to others. (Trust us, it's not as hard as you think! You can do it!)

# Index

# Index